THOMAS MORE
THROUGH MANY EYES

First published 1978
© Leighton Thomson 1978

Cover:
    SIR THOMAS MORE

    From the Holbein miniature.

Reproduced by kind permission of the Treasurer of Lincoln's Inn, the Lord
Widgery, P.C., O.B.E., T.D., D.L., Lord Chief Justice of England.

Copies of this book are obtainable from Leighton Thomson, 4 Old Church
Street, Chelsea, London, S.W.3, England, by whom it is published.

Printed in Great Britain by Bocardo & Church Army Press Ltd.,
Temple Road, Cowley, Oxford, England

To the memory of
Sir Thomas More
scholar, statesman, saint.

CONTENTS

Foreword Lord Hailsham of St. Marylebone
Lord High Chancellor 1970–74.

Preface

Preachers of the annual Thomas More Sermon at Chelsea
Old Church.

1. Norman Sykes, Dixie Professor of Ecclesiastical History, Cambridge

2. Edward Carpenter, Dean of Westminster

3. J. R. H. Moorman, Bishop of Ripon

4. F. J. Taylor, Bishop of Sheffield

5. J. W. C. Wand, Bishop of London

6. Geoffrey Lampe, Regius Professor of Divinity, Cambridge

7. C. W. Dugmore, Professor of Ecclesiastical History, London

8. R. L. P. Milburn, Master of the Temple

9. David Edwards, Canon of Westminster

10. Gordon Fallows, Bishop of Sheffield

11. Robert Stopford, Bishop of London

12. J. W. M. Vyse, Vicar of Aylsham, Norwich

13. Alfonso de Zulueta, Canon of Westminster Cathedral

14. A. L. Lawler, Vicar of St. Dunstan's, Canterbury

15. Howard Root, Professor of Theology, Southampton

16. Michael Ramsey, former Archbishop of Canterbury.

17. Stanley Greenslade, Regius Professor of Ecclesiastical History, Oxford

18. J. P. Hickinbotham, Principal of Wycliffe Hall, Oxford

19. Henry Cooper, Rector of Bloomsbury, London

20. J. C. Dickinson, Senior Lecturer in Theology, Birmingham

21. John McManners, Regius Professor of Ecclesiastical History, Oxford

22. L. W. Cowie, Senior Lecturer in History, Whitelands College, London

23. Alan C. Clark, Roman Catholic Bishop of East Anglia

24. Ian Thomson, Director of the Bible Reading Fellowship

25. Donald Coggan, Archbishop of Canterbury

Index

CHRONOLOGY

1478   Thomas More born in Milk Street, Cheapside (6 Feb)
1491   page to Archbishop of Canterbury (Morton) at Lambeth Palace
1492   to Oxford, Cathedral Hall—pupil of Linacre and Grocyn
1494   entered at New Inn
1496   removed to Lincoln's Inn
       reader at Furnivall's Inn
1504   Member of Parliament
1508   visited Louvain and Paris
1509   Bencher of Lincoln's Inn
1510   Under-Sheriff of London
1511   Reader of Lincoln's Inn
1515   an Envoy to Flanders
1516   published "Utopia"
1518   Master of Requests, and Privy Councillor
       welcomed Campeggio
1520   present at the Field of the Cloth of Gold
       built his house in Chelsea
1521   knighted
       Under-Treasurer to the King
       accompanied Wolsey to Calais and Bruges
1522   received grants of land in Oxfordshire and Kent
1523   Speaker of the House of Commons
1525   High Steward of Oxford and Cambridge Universities
       Chancellor of Duchy of Lancaster
1527   participated in negotiations with Wolsey at Amiens
1528   completed "Dialogue" (mainly against Tyndale)
       remodelled his south chapel in Chelsea Church
1529   succeeded Wolsey as Lord Chancellor
1532   resigned the chancellorship
       erected tomb in Chelsea Church
1534   committed to the Tower
1535   trial in Westminster Hall
       beheaded (6 July)

FOREWORD

OF the long line of Lord Chancellors, dating back to the days of Saxon England, three have been canonised as saints by the Roman Catholic Church. Of these three, Swithun, the rain maker, Thomas Becket, the "holy blissful martyr" of the Canterbury Tales, and Thomas More, murdered on the 6th July 1535, like Becket, by his sovereign, only More speaks to us in the language of today.

When More died on the scaffold, a shudder of horror ran through Christian Europe, comparable only to that felt at the death of Kings at the hands of their subjects, of Charles I of England, of Louis XVI of France, of Nicolas II of Russia. The Emperor himself sent for the English Ambassador and said that rather than lose so wise a councillor he would rather have been deprived of his finest city.

For More was an international figure. In an age when Latin was still the cultural language of the West, his works, secular and religious, had been printed in Germany and France, and were known there as widely as in his own country. His panegryic was penned by his intimate friend, Erasmus, the father of Christian humanism.

When a man dies in such a fashion for a scruple of conscience, as More did, the real hero is apt to be buried beneath hagiography. But More's sanctity, if he was a saint, can never quite cover up his earthy humanity.

To this day his living descendants bear witness to his refusal to adopt the celibate life of the Catholic priest. Though his wit was keen, his humour was coarse, even, at times by modern standards, almost lewd. Though, in the end, he died for his convictions, he was never without ambition. Undersheriff of London, barrister and Bencher of Lincoln's Inn, M.P., Speaker of the House of Commons, Lord Chancellor of England, here was a man of the world, immersed in politics, the frequenter of courts, the intimate of the sovereign who became his murderer.

His best known work, *Utopia,* has spawned an infinite number of progency; it creaated a new genre of literature, peculiarly English and probably neither Swift's *Gulliver,* nor H. G. Wells' *Men like Gods,* Huxley's *Brave New World,* nor Orwell's *1984* would have taken the form they did if More had not composed *Utopia,* and the very title, translated and reversed in English, reappears in Butler's *Erewhon.*

For long, More was too little honoured in his own country. Though a martyr to his beliefs, he was no prophet, But the smear of treason, of which he was falsely accused, dies hard. Though he was not the first layman to hold the office of Lord Chancellor, any more than Wolsey was the last cleric to do so, he was in a sense the first of the modern Chancellors, a politician, a judge, and a lawyer to his fingertips. As I pass along Chelsea embankment and see his statue seated outside the Church wherein he worshipped, now rebuilt after very severe damage in the war, I feel strangely humbled, neither as a lawyer, nor as a Christian worthy to have served in succession to so marvellous a man.

I hope this volume of sermons, preached in Chelsea Old Church in honour of his memory, reaches a wide public, and serves to inspire new admirers to the imitation of his learning, his integrity, his piety, and his wit.

HAILSHAM

House of Lords

PREFACE

WHEN Chelsea Old Church was severely bombed in 1941 it chanced that the part least damaged was the fourteenth century chapel which Sir Thomas More restored in 1528. During the rebuilding of the 1950's the congregation, worshipping in the More Chapel, was encouraged by the thought of following in the steps of this great churchman and parishioner of the village of Chelsea, and we have honoured his memory each year in a special sermon.

Readers of this book will be confirmed in their view that in Thomas More they recognize a man whose influence not only crosses frontiers but is seen increasingly to have world-wide significance.

I am greatly indebted to the authors of these addresses for their permission to publish them and to Lord Hailsham for his Foreword, and this is done as a contribution from Chelsea to the quincentenary of More's birth and to the ecumenical movement of the present time. We shall continue to welcome the many from all denominations who cherish More's memory and visit his church.

Chelsea Old Church
    Vicarage
4 Old Church Street,
Chelsea, London S.W.3.

C. E. LEIGHTON THOMSON

PROFESSOR NORMAN SYKES

DIXIE PROFESSOR OF ECCLESIASTICAL HISTORY IN THE UNIVERSITY OF CAMBRIDGE

4 JULY 1954

University of Leeds. Scholar Queens College Oxford. M.A. and D.Phil 1923. Select Preacher Cambridge 1933/41/46: Oxford 1942–44. Professor of History University College of S.W. Exeter 1931–33. University of London 1933–43. Canon Theologian of Liverpool Cathedral 1937–42. Fellow and Praelocutor Queens College Oxford 1943–45. Fellow Emmanuel College Cambridge from 1944. Proctor in Convocation University of Cambridge from 1945. D.D. 1949 F.B.A. 1951.

This sermon was delivered in the More Chapel which, happily, was that part of Chelsea Old Church which escaped with least damage in the bombing of 1941. Immediately after the bombing the congregation continued steadfastly in regular worship (in the building next-door) and returned to the More Chapel with its temporary extension on 2 July 1950.

The Chancel and Lawrence Chapel of Chelsea Old Church were re-hallowed by J. W. C. Wand, Bishop of London, on 4 MAY 1954.

12

1

Render unto Caesar the things that are Caesar's; and unto God the things that are God's. Mark. XII. 17.
The powers that be are ordained of God; therefore he that resisteth the power, withstandeth the ordinance of God. Romans. XIII. 1.
We ought to obey God rather than men. Acts. V. 29.

"HE was the first of any whatsoever layman in England that died a martyr for the defence and preservation of the unity of the Catholic Church. And that is his special, peerless prerogative". So wrote Nicholas Harpsfield of Thomas More; and in so writing, penetrated to the core of two problems which chiefly vexed his sixteenth-century contemporaries, namely the relationship of national churches to the universal church, and the position of the papacy in the catholic church. And it remains still, after more than four centuries, the peerless prerogative of More that, being himself a layman, he died in defence of the papal supremacy in the church, and in *defiance* of that movement of reform, which was characterised by its assertion of the rights of independent national churches against Rome, and therein of the place of the laity in general and of the Christian sovereign in particular, within the Catholic Church. Herein lies at once the nobility and tragedy of his death.

For all the elements of poignant tragedy are present in the life and death of Sir Thomas More. At the accession of Henry VIII, when More was just past his 31st birthday, England seemed on the threshold of a veritable golden age. The fair promise of the Renaissance, that revival of humanism and classical studies, of which More himself was a leader and prophet, seemed about to bear fruit, fully and richly, under the aegis of a young monarch, whose culture and chivalry were matched with the splendour of the times. The oecumenical scholar Erasmus hastened back from Rome to England to share in its trophies; and the friends of learning and the champions of reform alike, made ready for the twin triumph of their principles.

> Bliss was it in that dawn to be alive,
> But to be young was very heaven.

Yet before a quarter of a century had run its course, the breach with Rome had been effected, the Act of Supremacy had been passed requiring

13

acceptance of the king, instead of the pope, as supreme head on earth of the Church of England; and on 6 July 1535 More was beheaded for refusal to take the oath of supremacy. He had indeed resigned his office as Chancellor the very day after Convocation in 1532 had first accepted the royal supremacy; and the remainder of his years were but the ruthless and inexorable working out of the logic of this resignation. Humanist, scholar, legist, and layman; More died for the papal supremacy against that of the king, and for the monopoly of the church by the clergy against the new self-assertion of the laity. Truly he was 'a very gentil, parfait knight'

But it is an inescapable function and duty of the student of history to distinguish the *causes* from the *occasions* of the great movements which have changed the face and fortunes of empires and churches. The *occasion* of that breach with Rome, which opened the floodgates of reform both in doctrine and worship in England, was the tangled matrimonial history of Henry VIII; and the sordid, unworthy episode of his so-called "divorce" of Catherine of Aragon and marriage with Anne Boleyn has sullied the record of the beginnings of the English reformation. Judged from this personal standpoint indeed the contest between More and his sovereign was sadly unequal. Between their personal virtues there existed only the relationship of contradiction. Even so, Henry VIII's standards of conduct were little worse, if little better, than those of contemporary Roman popes. But his "divorce" was only the occasion of the reformation; and for its causes one must look beneath the surface and enquire more closely.

The cry for "the reform of the church in head and members" had been sounded and re-echoed indeed throughout western Christendom for at least a century before the accession of Henry VIII. The Conciliar Movement of the early fifteenth-century had marked an attempt to effect it by a return to the method of general councils, familiar in the fourth and fifth centuries of Christian history; and its failure had necessitated more drastic means. Where medicine had been in vain, surgery might be needful. It would be needless at this time to recite the thrice-told tale of abuses crying out for reform; of financial oppression, and of the association of the most sacred and intimate offices of religion with pecuniary gain. The researches of historians have accumulated an almost overwhelming case for reformation; nor was the need confined to a financial, judicial and administrative purge of the Roman curia. There was a strong and growing popular aversion to the multiplication of orbits and requiem Masses, and the consequent degradation of the order of priesthood. The only question was, not *whether,* but *when* and *how* reform would come.

The actual reformation enacted in English history was a complex movement, woven of many strands, not all of which were noble, disinterested, or spiritual; indeed the basest motives of human cupidity, greed, time serving, and downright blasphemy jostled shoulders with the

14

earnest desires of reformers. It was an ineradicable part of its tragedy that some individuals of saintly character and unsullied probity, such as Sir Thomas More and Bishop John Fisher, should have lost their lives in the confused melée, "as on a darkling plain

> Swept with confused alarms of struggle and flight,
> Where ignorant armies clash by night".

But is it the case that More was a confessor for God against Caesar, and because he held, with St. Peter, that we must obey God rather than men? Or was there something also to be said for the Pauline principle that the powers that be are ordained of God, in such wise that whoso resisteth the power, withstandeth the ordinance of God? Was More in fact the proto-martyr for the freedom of the Church against the modern totalitarian state *Leviathan* drunk with power and the blood of saints?

To state the issues thus is to simplify a complex situation too easily. One of the salient characteristics of the Reformation was its appeal away from the tradition of the church to the authority of the Bible. In no sphere was this appeal more potent than in that of political thought, of the relations of church and state. In the historical books of the *Old* Testament, the Reformers saw the pattern of government, as God himself had prescribed it to his chosen people; and there they beheld the prototype of "the godly prince" over all persons and in all causes as well ecclesiastical as civil within his kingdom, supreme. In the *New* Testament indeed they saw no Christian prince as yet emergent; yet even to the heathen emperors of Rome, St. Paul and St. Peter had commanded obedience on the part of Christians. How much more therefore could a Christian monarch require the *undivided* allegiance of his subjects? For, negatively, the reformers found in the new Testament no evidence at all for the claims of the Roman papacy to be Universal Ordinary over the whole church. They proclaimed therefore that the Christian sovereign, "the godly prince", was the legitimate heir to all the prerogatives of the Hebrew Kings, and that he was directly charged by God with the care of his people's spiritual welfare no less than their temporal prosperity.

In the very different political, social, and religious conditions of this 20th century, it is difficult to understand imaginatively and sympathetically the tremendous importance which our sixteenth century forebears attached to their theory of "the godly prince". But it is essential to the understanding of the reformation that we should realise that the royal supremacy was not understood as transgressing the crown rights of the Redeemer in his church (to adopt a very modern phrase). The king was not taking the place of Christ; but simply of the pope. Archbishop Whitgift in the reign of Elizabeth I thus stated the position. "If you mean the *universal* church, only Christ is the Head; neither hath He any vicegerent to supply that *universal* care over the *whole* church. But if you

15

speak of *particular* churches, as the church of England, the church of Denmark, then, as the prince is the chief head and governor of the commonwealth under God, so is he of the church likewise. For it is certain that the Christian magistrate hath as great authority as the magistrate had under the Law. But then the civil magistrates had the chief authority, both in matters of commonwealth and of the church also; therefore the magistrate ought to have the same now in like manner".

This principle of course was not peculiar to England. It applied also and equally to the kings of the Scandinavian countries, to the German Lutheran princes; and even to the Calvinist reformation as seen in the neighbouring kingdom of Scotland. There indeed no less redoubtable a figure than John Knox himself, asking the question, "whether the reformation of religion falling into decay and punishment of false teachers, do appertain to the civil magistrates and nobility of any realm", gave as his answer: "that the ordering and reformation of religion with the instruction of subjects, doth especially appertain to the civil magistrate, shall God's perfect ordinance, his plain word, and the facts and examples of those that of God are highly praised, most evidently declare". In this matter policy walked hand in hand with precept; for in practice the power and might of the papacy could not be challenged and overthrown by the spiritual force of religion, but only by the determination of the organised temporal power.

There is an old familiar Latin tag, *qualis rex talis grex;* like prince, like people; and the principle underlying the royal supremacy was not confined to kings. They were but representaitve of the laity in the church; and the second outstanding feature of the reformation was the successful attempt of the laity to break down the monopoly of the church hitherto possessed by the clergy. We are entirely mistaken if we think of church and state in the sixteenth-century, as we should naturally do today, as two distinct and separate societies, standing over against each other. Rather they were one and the same society, ruled by two distinct hierarchies of officials, the clergy and the laity. In the middle ages a "churchman" meant a cleric as distinct from a layman; and this meaning lingered on into Shakespeare's times. The reformation was a determined and successful campaign by the laity to insist on their rights within the church as against the clergy. In England this conflict and its issue were writ in so large letters, that even he who runs may read, in the events of the first year of Elizabeth I, a quarter of a century after Thomas More had died in defence of the papacy and the clergy. For in 1559 the purely clerical assembly of the Convocation of Canterbury passed six resolutions, one of which affirmed the necessity of the papal supremacy, and another formally denied the right of the laity to concern themselves with the definition of the faith, sacraments, and the discipline of the church. In reply, the parliament gave the retort courteous by passing the two Acts of Supremacy and Uniformity; and passing them despite the opposition of all the bishops present in the house of lords. By the first act the royal supremacy was restored and the papal headship abolished; and by the second, the laity ordered the use of an English Book of Common Prayer, in substance the same with that legally authorised today. Here was the lie direct to Thomas More; and if any doubt had lingered in the minds of Anglican churchmen as to the significance of their actions, the defenders of Rome speedily dissolved it. "In matters of faith", asked one of their propagandists, Thomas Stapleton, "shall we sever ourselves from our fathers and brethren (the whole corpus of Christendom beside) by the virtue of an Act passed by laymen only". When More asserted his peerless prerogative of being the first of any layman whatsoever to die for the papal headship and the clerical monopoly of the church, he shewed a singular prescience; for the two principals were indissolubly knit together. Shall two walk together except they be agreed: and the reformers made answer by asserting in their turn the royal supremacy and the rights of the laity.

But, it may be wearily asked, is not all this but the flowing of plaintive numbers "of old, unhappy far-off things and battles long ago"? Have these distant matters any relevance to our present condition, upon whom the ends of the ages are come? It must be answered boldly and confidently that the good estate of the Christian Church demands the possession and exercise still by the laity of their franchise and privilege as an essential party of that royal priesthood and holy nation, of which St. Peter wrote. To an enquirer who once asked Dr. Thomas Arnold, "what is the laity", he made the succint and sufficient rejoinder, "the church—minus the clergy". To a younger contemporary of his, Cardinal Manning, his Roman confidante Monsignor Talbot, wrote at a later date: "What is the province of the laity? To hunt, to shoot, to entertain; these matters they understand: but to meddle with ecclesiastical matters, they have no right at all". Sir Thomas More died for this latter conception of the place of the laity: the reformation stood for the former. Nor is it even now an outmoded or obsolete ideal. The Church in England today still lags far behind its sister Church of Scotland, and also behind most of the overseas Provinces of the Anglican Communion, in the duty of according to the laity their full measure of authority and responsibility in its deliberative and legislative assemblies.

But our own times have seen the rise of a much more formidable phenomenon, which threatens the entire fabric of Christian civilisation, the totalitarian state. Armed with unprecedented means both of controlling opinion by coercive measures and of moulding the minds of its subjects by broadcasting and other educational methods, it has set itself

17

in the place of God. For whether its political ideology be of the right or of the left, whether facist or communist, it is homogeneous in claiming all power and authority and demanding the absolute allegiance of its citizens. In place of the true religion revealed in the Hebrew and Christian dispensations, it sets up some secular ideology of its own devising; and logically therefore persecutes all religions based on divine revelation. Between the contemporary totalitarian state and that royal supremacy which Thomas More rejected, there is a great gulf fixed. For in the sixteenth-century it was axiomatic and fundamental that the sovereign was "the godly prince", or as our Prayer Book has it "our most religious and gracious king". There was no idea of a non-christian state challenging the authority of Christ in his church. In face of contemporary persecution and oppression, many Christians of all churches, catholic and protestant, clergy as well as laity, have laid down their lives; believing that they must needs obey God rather than men. For when Caesar openly and avowedly claims the things that are of God, no other course than resistance is possible. Perhaps in the lurid light of this modern persecution of Christianity, on a scale far vaster and to a degree much more thorough than anything undertaken by the Roman emperors, the moral of Thomas More's death may be a means of drawing together Christians of all persuasions in common defence against an universal adversary. For, whatever verdict we may pass on the justice of the case between the papal and royal supremacies of the sixteenth century, between the freedom of national churches and the Italianate monopoly of the see and court of Rome, between the identification of the clergy with the church and the assertion by the laity of their claim also to be churchmen, we may not doubt that in spirit and intention Thomas More was the forerunner of all who have laid down their lives for refusing to render unto Caesar the things that are God's. For on that 6th day of July 1535, "he spoke little before his execution. Only he asked the bystanders to pray for him in this world, and he would pray for them elsewhere. He then begged them earnestly to pray for the King, that it might please God to give him good counsel; protesting that he died the King's good servant, but God's first". "The king's good servant, but God's first"; what more succint and sufficient epitaph could a Christian citizen desire or deserve. For we ought to obey God rather than men.

CELT

CANON EDWARD FREDERICK CARPENTER

CANON OF WESTMINSTER ABBEY

3 JULY 1955

University of London. A.K.C. 1935. Fellow of Kings College London 1951. B.A. 1932, M.A. 1934, B.D. 1935, Ph.D. 1943. Canon of Westminster Abbey 1951–74: Treasurer 1959–74: Archdeacon of Westminster 1963–74. Dean of Westminster from 1974.

2

I TAKE as my text the introductory sentence used this morning—"The memory of the just is blessed".

When your Vicar asked me to preach this sermon, he reminded me that there was a long standing connection—not a very happy one I fear —between Westminster Abbey and Chelsea Old Church. It appears that in 1240 a very bitter quarrel developed between them as to the title to a salmon which was caught in the Thames: this was a quarrel between the Abbot of Westminster and the Rector of Chelsea Church. So unsettling was the dispute that it was referred to Pope Gregory IX and I have a faint suspicion that the cost of the legal fees involved far exceeded anything the Abbot would have got from that salmon caught in the Thames: but his *amour propre* was involved.

However, I can assure your Vicar that no such situation now exists; whether, because no salmon would dare to penetrate so far up, the river, or (as I should like to think), because people are more civilised these days. Let me very simply say that very harmonious relations now exist between these two old and ancient institutions.

Alexander Pope wrote that the best study of mankind is man. Most of us know what the poet meant and I think most of us would agree with him. We can enter into this study in various ways—through books, through the direct encounter when person meets person 'face to face'. The part of life which for most looms largest is that which arises out of people meeting people. Most of us are not particularly interested in ideologies, perhaps not so interested as we ought to be, but all of us are vitally and vividly interested in people. It is indeed the most profound of all experiences when one person breaks through into the living consciousness of another. Yet these personal relationships, if they are satisfying and most subtle, yet constitute the most difficult aspects of life to keep under control.

If the best study of mankind is man, for the Christian the paradox holds that the best study of the supreme reality of God is in the man Jesus. As we try to face up to the challenge implicit in his historic life we are not only made aware of that which lies deeply embedded within ourselves, the *imago dei,* but we are also brought into an understanding— so far as it is given to mortal man so to understand the Most High God. If

21

this is uniquely true of Jesus I believe it to be true of lesser mortals. It is through our personal understanding of them that God reveals himself in divers manners and many rôles.

If any of us has the privilege of knowing a really good person we not only discover something about the common humanity which we all bear, but something about the great God himself. Maybe if we were brought too immediately into the true light of God's presence we should be blinded by excess of light. So does he reveal himself through holy and humble men of heart—those who in mirroring the divine light refract it into a myriad of rays.

I do not need to remind you who worship Sunday by Sunday in this Church that, among such great men Sir Thomas More will for ever hold an honoured and respected place. It is my privilege this morning to say something about him as a living vital person: a person with like passions unto ourselves, sometimes troubled, often perplexed but never failing to be courageous. I want to bring Sir Thomas More before us as one through whom the glory of God shone, asking ourselves as we do so what his example can mean to us. It is but a commonplace to say that Sir Thomas lived in a very difficult, dangerous and explosive world; maybe in this respect it was not so unlike that which we know—an age of dangerous and unsettling transition. We ourselves live at the end of an age and we do not yet know the shape and pattern of things to come. When Sir Thomas More lived in Chelsea and went up daily to the City the world around him was in a state of uncertainty, confusion and ambiguity. The new jostled with the old. The established order was identified with the Roman Catholic Church and its authoritative teaching mission. Aristotle still dominated the philosophical schools. Yet an invigorating wind of change was blowing through the corridors of power. People were beginning to be more curious about human life and to ask great questions and in the process not to accept so easily the ancient dogmatic answers. The New Testament was beginning to be known in its original Greek and historically interpreted. The world had suddenly expanded as men traversed and peered through their telescopes into inter-stellar space. There was an excitement, an enlargement of life breaking through that which was traditional and familiar. Thus it was not easy for the men of that time to know exactly where they were. Anxious to go forward they were yet regretfully of the past.

The greatness of Thomas More was that he had the insight, the humility and most certainly the courage, to try to face up to the implications of this particular and ambiguous situation. There was much he felt that was good, healthy and worthwhile in these old traditions that men had inherited from a distant past, and which some excessive enthusiasts would

22

throw overboard lock, stock and barrel. Thus in some respects he was a great traditionalist, still looking to the past for inspiration and anxious not wantonly to break the cake of custom. On the other hand, Thomas More welcomed the new spirit embodied in the Renaissance, the wealth of new knowledge, and the discovery of the human culture of Greece.

Erasmus, More's friend, was buoyant with the great hope that this liberating spirit, illuminating the spirit of man, would lead to a fuller vision and a greater hope. More had a foot in both camps, though he was no compromiser affecting to be all things to all men. At one moment he seemed to be all humanist going the way of Erasmus, at another all traditionalist committed to preserving in its essentials the religious structure of medieval Europe freed of its abuses. He wished to retain what was best in the old, and equally pioneer the new. He did not wish to be irrationally conservative or impetuously reformist.

In his freedom from prejudice, in his steady courage to hold on to past treasures, and yet go boldly forward, he has a message for us living in and through an equally uncertain and ambiguous age. We know perfectly well that the revolution in 'life-styles' during the last fifty years is extreme and that consequently there is a tendency to regard everything old as perverse and naive, or everything new as wicked and dangerous. There is a via media and Sir Thomas More sought it out and remained true to it when found.

The essential greatness of Thomas More does not lie only in his freshness of spirit, his wit and liveliness, his intellectual brilliance; but also in that which changed Thomas More, Lord Chancellor, into St. Thomas More. That is his own deep personal integrity. To remain true to one's conscience is, in the last analysis, the one thing needful. Sir Thomas More lived in a world which was in many respects shockingly cruel, dominated by a sadistic monarch, whose precise motivation must, in entirety, remain a mystery.

In such days Sir Thomas More, in season and out of season, endeavoured to remain true to his God to whom he believed that final allegiance should be given. He saw the policy of Henry VIII as the breaking up of western Christendom, and the introduction of lawlessness into a divinely instituted order.

Thus he surrendered power and resigned his office of Lord Chancellor in 1532. He refused to take the oath required of him under the Act of Succession and was committed to the Tower.

No man originally had a greater admiration for Sir Thomas More than Henry VIII. He found him entertaining, and a scholar; he appreciated his high intelligence and the influence he could exercise in the seats of

23

power. But the cost to More of continuing to enjoy royal favour was personal prostitution. Here Wolsey represents a sad contrast.

I would remind you of the tenderness and simplicity of More's life lived here in Chelsea in a commodious and spacious house. It is indeed a moving testimony to a man who had been Lord Chancellor and thus tasted power that he could find happiness surrounded by his large family of three generations and great joy in their intimate and personal relationship. How many great men suffering such pressures could have relaxed as he did. "There is no man living so affectionally as he and he loveth his old wife as if she were a girl of sixteen", so said Erasmus. "He is as cheerful and well blessed as if the best thing possible had been done to him. His house at Chelsea is a veritable school of Christian relation". There are not many great men about whom this could be said with full truth.

Finally it was his deep personal integrity which led More to the most fateful decision of his life—his opposing the Act of Supremacy, by which Henry was made supreme head of the Church. In the deepest recesses of his conscience, More felt he could not subscribe. Thus He went, we might say, clinically to his death. Many, including his family, thought that he was being over scrupulous: that it was really his duty to keep himself alive as the only man who could really influence the King: but he just could not see it this way. On 6th July, 1535, he was beheaded on Tower Hill.

One thing Thomas More certainly had in common with Luther. When the crisis came he was able to say, "Here I stand, I can do no other, so help me God". This is the final test of any man—to hang on, at all costs, to the vision which God has given him and to affirm, "here is the point of no return. I am irrevocably committed come what may".

Whenever I think of More my mind instinctively moves to Cardinal Wolsey, a man of great qualities who prostituted tremendous talents to serve a tyrannical king—a king who, after loading honours upon him, suddenly broke him. Alone and in the supreme bitterness of disillusion Shakespeare makes Wolsey cry—, "Had I but served my God with half the zeal I served my King he would not, in mine age, have left me naked to mine enemies".

How different with Sir Thomas More. He did not feel abandoned on the scaffold at Tower Hill.

So today we can, in truth thank God for a humanist, a family man, and a very humble and devout follower of our Lord Jesus Christ.

24

THE REVEREND JOHN RICHARD HUMPIDGE MOORMAN

PRINCIPAL OF CHICHESTER THEOLOGICAL COLLEGE

1 JULY 1956

Emmanuel College Cambridge. M.A. 1931, B.D. 1941, D.D. 1945. Select Preacher University of Cambridge 1944: University of Oxford 1963. Hon.D.Litt. 1964. Birkbeck Lecturer Trinity College Cambridge 1948–49. Principal of Chichester Theological College and Chancellor of Chichester Cathedral 1946–56. Consecrated Lord Bishop of Ripon 1959: Resigned 1975. F.S.A. 1961. Delegate-observer to Second Vatican Council 1962–65. Member of the Anglican-Roman Catholic International Commission from 1969.

3

TWO texts this morning: the first from the fourth chapter of the Epistle to the Ephesians, the first verse—"I, therefore, the prisoner of the Lord, beseech you that ye walk worthy of the vocation wherewith ye are called." Second from I Corinthians 7. 20—"Let every man abide in the same calling wherein he is called."

In the Epistle to the Ephesians St. Paul shares with us his vision of the Church. He calls it the Body of Christ, thereby indicating that it is Christ's living agent, the instrument through which His Will is made effective. Such is the purpose of a body.

I have come here this morning in order to transfer from my mind to your minds certain thoughts. I have no means of doing this except by the use of my body: the feet to get me here, the tongue to speak and so on. Without the body's co-operation I should be helpless. And so Christ, who would communicate with men, needs a body; and that body is the Church. As the human body is made up of many parts, each with its own function and office, so is also the body of Christ.

So you see that if Christ wishes to make himself known to the people of Africa or Melanesia, it is through his body, the Church. If he wishes to proclaim to the world some truths or to communicate some thought to an individual soul it is through his body, the Church, that it is done. Each member of the body of Christ has, therefore, a great responsibility. And St. Paul reminds us of this in our first text—"I beseech ye that ye walk worthy of the vocation wherewith ye are called."

The thing which we most demand of our bodies is obedience. If our eyes do not open when we tell them to, then we cannot see and are helpless. If our legs will not support us when we desire to go somewhere, then we fall to the ground. If the body fails in obedience then the mind, the will is frustrated and crippled. So it is with the body of Christ. If the will of Christ is to be fulfilled, then within his body there must be obedience, and that depends upon health, harmony and the co-operation of each part.

The whole thing, each individual member and unit, working together with all other units is the creation of a living and active mechanism or instrument for the carrying out of the Divine Purpose. So St. Paul speaks of the Church being fitly framed together, each part to form a habitation of God in the Spirit. As with the human body, so with the body of Christ. It is made up of many different parts, but each must discover and fulfil its own particular function, otherwise there can be only chaos and weakness and frustration.Just as no intelligent person tries to write with his eyes or see with his toes, so within the body of Christ every man must fulfil his special function, that and no other. For a man to try to excercise some function which is outside his special vocation, the thing that God is calling him and intends him to do, is the way to disaster.

And so to our second text. In this St. Paul says "Let every man abide in the same calling wherein he is called." Only thus can the Church of God obey the divine commands and carry out the divine will. But before we leave the Epistle to the Ephesians, there is just one other point. St. Paul names some of the different types which make up the body of Christ. Some, he says, are called to be apostles and some prophets, some evangelists and some pastors and teachers; men with special gifts dedicated to special tasks, bringing their ability and skill to the service of God. So today, in the Church, we have bishops, priests, deacons, catechists, organists and choirmen, churchwardens and sidemen, teachers, missionaries, prison and hospital chaplains, treasurers and secretaries, vergers and sextons, each doing his essential part in the harmonious, healthy and effective working of the body of Christ.

It is the whole Church which acts together in the work of God, and thus the fulfilment of the divine will demands the existence of a body, the Church, and that body demands the existence of a large number of people, men and women, lay and clerical, learned and simple, good, bad and indifferent, who in their various ways are going to carry out the work of ministering and build up the body of Christ.

And I think you will see from this where I am trying to lead you this morning, and it is first of all to show you the immense importance in the Church of God, of the layman. People still talk sometimes of a man "going into the Church" as if the clergy were in the Church and everybody else was outside it. What perfect nonsense that is. What arrogant sacerdotalism. And yet it is a phrase which is still sometimes used. Of course the priesthood is vital. The calling of the priest is one of the greatest vocations which God can give to a man. Of course the Church needs those who can be its leaders, who are specially trained to teach, to tend, to guide, to admonish, to carry out the ministry of reconciliation and to lead men in the worship cf God. But the Church does not, and should not, ultimately depend upon its clergy. Christ needs every part of his body. He requires each man and woman to play his or her part in carrying out the work in which he has given to them. But as there are about a thousand laymen to every one priest in the Church then obviously it is upon the laity that the greatest responsibility rests. It is here that the quality of the Church's life will be decided. It is here that the effectiveness of the Church's work will be determined. What can be more inspiring to those outside her or to the infidel than the good layman—faithful, conscientious, courageous and prayerful, taking his full part in the worship of the church, ready to guide by his counsel and wisdom, anxious to use all his gifts in the service of God, witnessing in every department of life to the faith that is in him?

There is no limit to what the faithful layman can do and the Church owes much, more perhaps than is sometime realised, to its laymen.

We are here to-day to pay tribute to a very famous layman—Sir Thomas More, who worshipped here and loved this place more than 400 years ago. If we could travel back through time and see him as he was, we should see first of all, a noble and outstanding member of the state, whose life was devoted to the service of the community. He had at one time in his youth the idea of ordination, but he found this was not his vocation and turned to the law. He soon became a person of great importance— Under-treasurer, Speaker of the House of Commons and Lord Chancellor.

As we look at him in his work we are struck by his honesty and integrity. He lived in a changing world. A world in some ways rather like our own. Old things were being done away, old ideas and old standards abandoned. New men were rising to the top. Men on the make, unscrupulous, pushing, self-confident. In all this rather shabby crowd, Thomas More stands out for his uprightness, his high standards, his honesty and his purity. Sometimes it is said nowadays that politics is a dirty business. I don't know and I hope not. But no doubt similar things were said in his day. But there was no dirt where Thomas More was concerned.

In his younger days he had worked out his picture of what the ideal state would be—his Utopia. It was founded upon four cardinal virtues which Plato had long ago formulated: wisdom, fortitude, temperance and justice. Without these no state can survive for long. Their existence depends upon the type of person of whom the state is composed and especially upon the type of its leaders.

Thomas More set a high standard before his colleagues and fellows, for he was something more than just a lawyer, administrator and statesman, he was also a first class scholar and thinker. He had been well trained at Oxford and he lived on friendly terms with the greatest scholars of his day. His age was an age of scholarship. The new learning had broadened men's minds and broken down many old barriers. It was in the light of his scholarship, the breadth of his mind, the power of his imagina-

29

tion that he could see where the Church's weakness lay. Thomas More was a great believer in reform, though he was very critical of most of the reformers, who, he thought, were reckless in destroying so much that was good as well as what was bad. Reform was in the air. The trouble was that when it came, it came in the wrong way.

The greatest tragedy of Church history was the failure of the Church to reform itself in the later Middle Ages. Things were allowed to go on so long and get so bad that there came a point when men could bear it no longer. The new wine of the Renaissance burst the old bottles of medieval conservatism and indifference. And so in the sixteenth century we get, indeed, some reformation; but with it also disintegration. The great western Church which had been the strongest and most beneficial power in the world burst asunder, and in the place of unity we were left with what the prayerbook calls "our unhappy divisions".

There were many who were not at all grieved to see this happen. Some thought, perhaps rightly, that the Church had lost the power of self-reform and that nothing less than separation and a new start would make reform possible. Others clung to the idea of a unity, a christendom; and, while longing for reform, regarded division as the greater evil of the two. Thomas More was among the latter. And by way of making his contribution to reform he did not go about complaining of others, he started with himself and his own life. Here at least was something which every true churchman could do.

More's life was a life of severe discipline. He lived in an age of ostentation, the age of the Field of the Cloth of Gold. Sir Thomas was a man of great simplicity and austerity. His household was run on almost monastic lines, like Little Gidding a century later. He himself rose each day at two o' clock and prayed until seven. He had Mass every day. He had books of devotion read aloud at meal-times. He organised his household on lines of strict discipline in which duty to God took first place. Apart from the laying down of his life in what he believed to be the cause of God, Sir Thomas More has other claims to the title of saint, which is now accorded him.

"Walk worthy of the vocation wherewith ye are called." "Let every man abide in the same calling wherein he is called." Within the Church, as we saw, are many members each with his own function. Sir Thomas More was convinced, as St. Paul had been, that the well-being of the Church demanded that each member should do his own job faithfully and obediently and try not to interfere with rights and responsibilities which belonged elsewhere. He was the perfect layman. He loved the Church and served it faithfully, but he never tried to go outside his own sphere. It was on this point that he made his stand against the King, and it was for this principle that he laid down his life.

To Sir Thomas More, the divinely appointed head of the Church on earth was the Pope, the successor of St. Peter, the Vicar of Christ. He had his special function and clearly one of peculiar importance. He might fail, as often happened, but that made no difference to his vocation, his place in the divine plan for the world. Henry VIII was king, and as such had his special function. That also was an extremely important one, for the well-being of many depended on him. So long as Henry did his job and fulfilled his vocation according to the will of God he would have no more loyal supporter than Sir Thomas More. But when Henry tried to claim for himself titles and the rights which God had bestowed elsewhere and to call himself Supreme Head of the English Church, then More knew that he must protest whatever the cost.

Sir Thomas More was the ideal layman, who saw more clearly than most of us what the nature of the Church should be. He saw that God had called some to be apostles and some prophets and some pastors, teachers and some bishops and popes. He saw also that God had called some to be kings and statesmen, and in every other walk of life. But he also saw that if the true relationship between priest and layman is destroyed it can bring nothing but ruin and sorrow. So strongly did he feel this that he was prepared to defy a headstrong, cruel and violent monarch, knowing that the outcome of his defiance must be death.

We who have met together to-day in this fragment of the Church which he loved in order to do him honour, pay to him our tribute of respect and admiration.

The world always honours courage, not least that moral courage which is prepared to suffer for what it believes to be right. We shall, I hope, take away with us from this act of remembrance and praise a firmer resolve to walk worthy of the vocation wherewith we are called, to carry out with renewed zeal and sanctification the work which God has given us to do. For that, I feel, would be the message which Sir Thomas More would wish to put into our hearts to-day.

THE REVEREND FRANCIS JOHN TAYLOR

PRINCIPAL OF WYCLIFFE HALL, OXFORD

7 JULY 1957

Scholar Queens College Oxford. M.A. 1938
Chaplain Corpus Christi College Oxford
1939. Tutor and Lecturer Wycliffe Hall
Oxford 1938–42. Proctor in Convocation
Chester 1945–54. Lecturer St. Aidan's
College 1944–45 and 50–54. William Temple
College Hawarden 1947–53. Select Preacher
University of Edinburgh 1951: University of
Aberdeen 1952; University of Oxford 1961.
Principal of Wycliffe Hall 1955–62. Proctor
in Convocation Oxford 1955–62. Consecrated
Lord Bishop of Sheffield 1962.

4

IN the first chapter of St. Mark's Gospel, and verse 17, the words: "Jesus answering said unto them: 'Render therefore unto Caesar the things that are Caesar's and unto God the things that are God's.' And they marvelled at him".

Just four and a quarter centuries have passed since that early July morning when in the sight of a great crowd of spectators Thomas More accomplished his great act of dying. It can only be put that way because for a year previously he had been placed in that grim lodging of the Tower and there had prepared himself, as indeed at times earlier in his life he had prepared himself, for his last end. Those were hard and cruel days. There were many others who suffered in like manner during this same reign of King Henry VIII. Human flesh seemed cheaper then than it is now. Despite that fact, a thrill of horror went through this country and a good deal of Europe at the news that Thomas More had been executed, that he who had been the great servant of the King and of the country and, in a measure, the friend of the King, had been brought to so bitter and humiliating an end.

He was universally loved and respected for his great qualities of character, for his courteousness and meekness of bearing, for his learning, the care that he exercised over his family and household and for the beauty and attractiveness of his character. How then did it come that such a person, so respected, so highly regarded in wide circles and so honoured in Church and State, how did it come that such a person met the common end of a criminal? The words which I have given you as text may give at any rate some portion of the answer. "Render therefore to Caesar the things that are Caesar's and unto God the things that are God's".

Thomas More thought of himself as he drew near to this dread end as rendering to Caesar that which Caesar could claim—his body—and to God that which God alone could claim—his immortal soul. If then we ask ourselves, which we should on an occasion like this, what the point is of commemorating such a person whose world, whose outlook, whose thoughts were so different from ours, we may begin to answer by saying that there are nevertheless certain important lessons in his life and career which we forget in our day and in our so different circumstances at our peril.

To begin with, this. Quite plainly in the words of our Lord, Caesar stands as a symbol for the State, whether at the centre or in local government and it has a proper authority and has a proper claim which he may make upon us all. Our Lord was ready during his ministry and in the answer which he gave to those who presented such a teasing question, to acknowledge that, fully and explicitly. So also as a good disciple and follower of his Lord was Thomas More four centuries ago. His own inclinations would have moved him towards a life of quiet scholarship, of work in the law and of care for his family and household, but he was not allowed to remain in such a comparatively obscure walk of life. Instead his reputation as a man of integrity, a man of attractive personality brought him under the notice of wider circles until eventually it brought him into the service of the King himself. For though it was contrary to his own personal inclinations, More was sufficiently recollected of the teaching and example of his Lord not to be able to refuse the summons to go and serve in that fashion. He left his own legal practice and went directly to the service of the King for nearly a dozen years. it meant of course even in the somewhat leisured circumstances of those days, that he was much pressed with business and little able to give the time and attention to his home here in Chelsea that he would gladly have done. It was indeed a sacrifice for him as the public service, whether at church or state, is bound to impose a measure of personal sacrifice on those who undertake it in our day. That he was under obligation to do this, he recognised: Caesar had a just claim upon him and he sought to answer that claim. Whatever he was required to do which was in accord with law and justice he strove to accomplish, and earned in so doing the high regard of the other servants of the King and of the King himself and of monarchs overseas. At the same time More was mindful of the second half of our text: "Render unto God the things that are God's" and he was clear from the beginning that important and far-reaching as is the authority of Caesar, it is a limited authority. Caesar exercises his authority by divine permission and if he exceeds his lawful given authority then he is in due course answerable to God for the misuse of the power entrusted to him and it may come that Christian men and women will have to refuse Caesar when he exceeds his lawful authority. In the view of Thomas More there came a moment when Caesar exceeded his lawful authority. How you determine this fact where Caesar exceeds his lawful authority is bound to differ from age to age and as circumstances change. We cannot now see the problems in quite the same light in which More saw them four hundred years ago. At the least we have to recognise that there were serious problems and problems of conscience for him and for others. He was quite clear that Caesar was exceeding his authority, that there had come a point at which God's law was being invaded and broken by the tyrannous act of a king and a parliament under the pressure of that autocratic will, and he had no

34

option but to resist at that point. His resistance was quiet and orderly and peaceable. He was no flaming revolutionary. He was no person to rally to his banner a disorderly rabble and lead them to attack the places of authority. He was not even of the sort to stand in some public place and issue a flaming act of defiance, and he was not willing to give his assent to that which he believed to be contrary to the law and will of God.

As far as possible he avoided giving offence. He sought in the words of the new Testament to live peaceably with all men. But all men would not allow him to live at peace with them. And here particularly is where that age touches ours. The autocratic power of the King was not content to allow More to slip out of sight and quietly carry on his family life and merely not to give assent to that which the King required of his subjects. Efforts were made to probe into the faults, into the secret motives and ideas of the heart of More and others of his contemporaries.

Reading about the methods which were adopted for pressing into secret places of the personality reminds one of some of the terrible things we read in our day of the brain-washing of victims of political persecution. The men of four centuries ago may have conducted their methods a little bit differently but they were not wholly ignorant of this terrible art of brain-washing and of putting pressure upon the inner personalities of men and women. It was at this point particularly that More found himself under an inescapable obligation to resist.

"I do no man harm," he said "and I say none harm and I wish none harm. I wish all men well. Why then do you push me to this point?" and realising that at the end of the time of his imprisonment and examination was almost certainly death he added the rather pathetic phrase "Would God that my death would benefit my Lord the King." He showed in that way the true spirit of a Christian martyr. Not one who foolishly and defiantly runs on death. One who, on the contrary, would follow the admonition of the Lord that when they persecute you in one city, flee to another. But there comes a time when we are unable to flee to another city, when we have to take our stand for that which we see to be right. We may of course be in error and no man can rightly go beyond that point of being obedient to his conscience and so More was brought to that point where he had no option but to resist, because in his view the law of God was being broken and the will of God invaded. And humbly, quietly, persistently, he gave his testimony at that point and laid down his life to establish the principle embodied in the words of Our Lord in the text that besides rendering what is truly Caesar's to Caesar we have always and at all times to render to God what is God's.

Like More, for those whose responsibilities carry them directly in the sphere of the service of Caesar, it is rarely, if ever, an easy decision to take—where the boundary comes and whether or no some particular action is disloyalty to God though it may be obedience to Caesar. And so it is in the way that More has a word to speak to us still over the centuries because in our day, particularly, Caesar has been making more and more claims upon men and women in this world. We are accustomed to think particularly of countries on the other side of the Iron Curtain as making ruthless and totalitarian demands upon the bodies and the souls of men and women and perhaps those demands are made in that part of the world more evidently and more ruthlessly than appears here. Caesar makes his demands here also. There are times when he comes very near to exceeding his lawful authority and we have to be quick and alert always to be clear that his is a limited authority and God alone may claim unlimited authority and unlimited allegiance and obedience from us, and that loyalty to God may bring us into the place where we must refuse the demands of Caesar. For More, loyalty to God and his will as he understood it, meant loyalty to the One Holy Catholic Church. Again we see this matter rather differently from the way in which he inevitably saw it more than four centuries ago. It is not without point to recall that in our day we are more and more concerned about the disunity of Christian people, about the scandal that that fact offers to the world and about the need for Christians everywhere to recognise their fellow Christians in different traditions and to draw closer together. The life and death of More were accomplished at a time when the old pattern of Christian unity was being broken up but the western world was changing from its medieval order to its modern order and the one Christendom or rather the ideal of Christendom in which men should live in a common state and in a common church was being subjected to intolerable pressures. He tried to serve the old ideal of the unity of Christian people and of the unity of Christian faith. For him that could be nothing else than continuing obedience to the See of Rome. Because as members of the Church of England we believe that the demands and methods of the See of Rome are inconsistent with primitive and biblical Christianity we have to disallow those claims. At the same time we cannot be anything else but quick and urgent in our concern about Christian unity and in our way to admire and approve the stand which More tried to make in a day of hardship and difficulty for the true unity of Christian people. And if he has anything to say to us at the present time on this point let us heed what it is he has to say and give ourselves afresh to seeking by prayer, by actions in so far as it is open to us and in any other way to the recovery of the broken unity of the Body of Christ. This testimony which he gave to the supremacy of God over Caesar and to the true unity of men and women in the faith of Christ was manifest also in his personal love. There are many pieces of evidence to show the beauty and the attractiveness of the domestic life which he ordered here in this part of the world. He was a great Christian who

36

sought in every way possible to follow the example of his Master. A man who disciplined himself and governed his household wisely and well. Indeed, in the midst of the pressing duties of state which fell upon him, he never failed to see that a proper space was found in his life for meditation and for prayer.

I believe that there are few things more needed in our day in the hurry and bustle of our life and in the almost intolerable pressures that come upon public men than that we should again find spaces of quiet, oases of meditation and prayer in which truly we may come into living touch with the very fountain source of our life in God himself and so find that unfailing strength and quietness and courage to pursue our way whether that way be in obscure place or high-lifted up in the public places of our land. So it is good for us to think back and to commemorate this great man. If we cannot, as indeed we cannot, think in the same way as he did and take exactly the same decisions as he did, principles which he faced and which he sought to fulfil are plainly principles of immediate and urgent importance for us all at the present day. The Christian church needs again in this country, as it is having to do in other parts of the world at the present time, to heed the words of the Master: Render therefore unto Caesar the things that are Caesar's but unto God the things that are God's.

THE RIGHT REVEREND AND RIGHT HONOURABLE JOHN WILLIAM CHARLES WAND, K.C.V.O., D.D., D.LITT.

CANON RESIDENTIARY OF ST. PAUL'S CATHEDRAL

6 JULY 1958

St. Edmund Hall Oxford B.A. 1907. M.A. 1911, D.D. 1934, Hon Fellow 1938, D.Litt. 1949, K.C.V.O. 1955, Fellow Kings College London 1956, Select Preacher University of Oxford 1930–32. Fellow Tutor and Dean of Oriel College Oxford 1925–34. University Lecturer in Church History Oxford 1931–34. Consecrated Lord Archbishop of Brisbane 1934. Translated to Bath and Wells 1943. Translated to London 1945. Resigned 1955. Dean of the Chapels Royal 1945–55. Prelate to the Most Excellent Order of the British Empire 1946–55. Canon Residentiary and Treasurer of St. Paul's Cathedral, London 1956–69.

Chelsea Old Church was re-consecrated by H. C. Montgomery Campbell, Bishop of London, in the presence of Her Majesty Queen Elizabeth The Queen Mother on 13 MAY 1958.

5

The Lord is My Light—Dominus illuminatio mea. Psalm 27. verse 1.

IT is the motto of the University of Oxford and it covers very admirably the life of this son of Oxford of whom we are thinking today. It covers his thought and his character, even although he was not enough of an Oxford man to stay the course. Why Thomas More came down without a degree is a matter for debate, but the probable reason was that the new thought had occasioned so great a revolution in the climate of opinion, that his father thought it desirable to bring him down before he was completely and finally contaminated.

It is necessary to try to understand the state of mind of his generation if we are to place Sir Thomas More in his rightful niche in the history of human thought and of the life of our country. It was a period of world revolution which was not entirely unlike the days in which we live. Just as today we have made an entirely new conquest of the air, so in the days of Thomas More discoverers had made a conquest of new worlds. The stories of Amerigo Vespucci were regularly studied and retold; the voyage of Columbus was even recognised to be as important as it actually turned out to be.

But this new physical conquest and discovery was by no means solitary. It coincided with a tremendous revolutionary movement in the sphere of thought. The return to the old classical literature of Greece and Rome had been assisted by the acquisition of new manuscripts of Greek origin that had flooded Europe after the conquest of Constantinople by the Turks. These things had started a ferment in the minds of men. They were no longer prepared to accept things merely on authority. They felt there were whole new worlds of study lying open before them and just as they had become adventurous beyond the seas, so they became adventurous in the realm of ideas.

In Italy, which was the *fons et origo* of the movement, this had led to a certain amount of revolutionary conduct, inspired by a *joie de vivre* that had undermined the old restraints and traditions. Further North, there was a more solid and serious outcome. The people applied essentially the same attitude of mind to the study of the Bible, the traditions of the

39

Church, the essence of religion, as in the South they had applied to the method of life and the conduct of contemporary man. And it was that adventurous spirit which was characteristic of the age, as I think indeed it is of our own age. I would go so far as to say that the main difference between the two ages is simply this: that at that period they felt everything lay in front of them and they were entirely unconscious of the dangers. Today too we feel that everything lies in front of us, but we are haunted by the terrible fear that in exploiting the new worlds opening out before us, we may destroy each other from the very face of the earth. And to that extent I think the age of Thomas More had the advantage of ours.

More was regarded himself as a typical member of this new kind of life and his writings give testimony to the fact that this is a sound judgment. He started, so it is said, the vogue of biographical literature in this country, which has come to its flower and consummation in our day. His life of Richard III is sometimes said not to have been by him at all, but by his great patron, Cardinal Morton, who wrote it in Latin; so it is suggested More was responsible merely for the translation. But whether that is so or not, the fact is that it is in itself a refined piece of English literature, which as English owes its origin to More, and which did set a style of future generations. His better-known work, *Utopia*, gives equal evidence of the new ferment of thought. And once again his genius starts a whole new type of literature; what he himself had derived from Plato's Republic and from Augustine's City of God, he hands on with new inspiration to future generations. All the studies of possible new worlds that we have had from his day right down to the period of H. G. Wells and beyond, are the result of the inspiration given by Thomas More.

But you and I, keeping his memory in reverence, are I imagine much more interested in his general attitude towards life and his theological position than we are in his influence either upon the constitution of the country or upon the history of our literature. I have said that the revolution in men's thoughts set people here in Northern latitudes rethinking the meaning of the Bible, the doctrine of the Church and the whole position of religion. More was fortunate in being accompanied in this particular kind of investigation by his two friends, Colet and Erasmus; the three men together we know as the Oxford Reformers. What they were really after is told us quite plainly and in unmistakable words by Erasmus himself, who, describing the work of Colet, said that what he did was to clear away the briars and the thickets with which the Gospel message had been overgrown so that people could see the essential meaning of the Gospel. And describing his own work, Erasmus said that what he himself had been trying to do was to bring out to public notice the essence of religion so as to reduce it to its fewest and its simplest principles.

Now I believe that although he nowhere says so, More was inspired by precisely the same kind of idea. He wished to clear away the confusion of the many details and complications in which the great medieval scholastics had involved the living essence of the Christian religion. But he, reducing it to the simplest possible principles, stated quite clearly a principle which is not stated with anything like the same directness and vividness by either of his great companions. More may have had the same kind of interests as they had in Biblical studies and in Church history, but as a lawyer he was much more interested than even they were in the contemporary constitutional situation of religion. And the most revealing sentence he ever uttered consisted of the few words, "The Pope holdeth up all".

Now this was no *obiter dictum*, the light expression of a trenchant opinion on the part of More; he was a person who had studied the situation with considerable thoroughness. It was probably he who had more than any other person to do with the writing of Henry VIII's thesis on the Seven Sacraments against Luther, the volume which won for Henry VIII the title of Defensor Fidei, still held by the monarchs of our country. And Henry VIII was himself no mean student of theology; so that the theological principles involved were thoroughly understood by More.

Again, he had himself written a dialogue against Tyndale. There he shows himself in not quite such a favourable and amiable light as he generally did, because after the manner of the age he could become very heated and even scurrilous in controversy. In any case he trounced Tyndale for what he believed to be his mistranslation of many passages in the Bible. So again More had studied the situation from the foundations. And of course he had here in London himself lectured on Augustine's City of God, for a considerable period, which meant that he had had to make himself thoroughly familiar with this basic work which was funda- mental for the whole development of medieval life and thought; a book that touches upon so many subjects and is the outcome of so great a genius that even to read it is a liberal education. And to study it, as More had to do in order to lecture upon it, means he must have had not merely a thorough grounding but a very adequate training in the theological problems of the time.

As a result, when he was involved in all the subsequent difficulties, in the last resort More pins his faith to this one great principle, that "the Pope holdeth up all". In enunciating it, More anticipated what seems to me to be the essence of modern Roman Catholic apologia.

It is interesting to notice how in recent years the cry "Rome never changes" has been dropped. With it has gone the whole system of defence

41

which asserted that what Rome teaches and practices today she has taught and practised from the beginning. Newman's teaching on development is at last having its effect on Roman theology. Obviously if there is development, one must have some standard or norm by which to decide whether the development is on the right lines or not. Anglicans are content to rest upon the creeds, the councils and above all the Bible. Rome has a less complicated judge. In the last resort the only thing that really matters is the decision of the Pope. And by that is meant the reigning Pope. Even if his decision appears to run counter to those of his predecessors he is still the Vicar of Christ and his voice must prevail.

But this was not the principle generally accepted at the time. There was indeed a contrary principle that was becoming much more widely accepted and had already become the gospel of the newly important middle class: "the King holdeth up all". It came with the new attention to the Bible from the Old Testament emphasis on the sanctity of the Lord's Anointed. It was reinforced by the Lutheran doctrine of the "godly prince". But it was aided most of all by the abounding vitality of Henry VIII himself. With his quick brain and physical prowess, his bounding ambition and ruthless drive, he exactly suited the people of the new age in which man had discovered a fresh mastery over his environment. It was this that enabled Henry to establish an absolute monarchy founded on the affection of his people. Presently this Tudor absolution was to develop in to the Stuart axiom of the divine right of Kings to govern wrong.

More already felt himself in this climate of opinion, as can perhaps be seen in the obsequiousness with which in prison he spoke of "the benefits and honours that he [the King] hath still from time to time most bountifully heaped upon me", and of his gracious consideration in promising to allow More's family to be present at his funeral. But the man who had had the courage to oppose both the present King and his father had nothing like the same innate respect for the sacredness of monarchy that was to cause a thinker like Cranmer such intense urgency of indecision in a few years time. At least where religion was concerned there could be in More's view no clash between the two authorities. The Pope was first and the King nowhere. The tragedy was that in his anxiety over his marriage the King had been forced through the exigencies of papal politics to usurp a place in the national religion which was readily acceded to the monarch by the new thought on the continent but which was clean contrary to More's fundamental beliefs. More took a stand which by the law of the land, however enacted, made him a traitor; and so he had to die.

Today we are naturally inclined, whatever our religious or political views, to follow the example of the Roman Church and canonise the martyr. We must however realise as historians that the issue did not seem so clear-cut in Thomas More's own day. People were not then so enamoured of individual religious liberty. If to many men of thought the needs of the state seemed paramount, simpler men thought it a plain duty to obey the King. Dame Alice, More's own wife, could not understand what her husband was so obstinate about, and if his favourite daughter, Margaret, showed more understanding and sympathy, she too added her weight to that of those who sought to deflect him from his purpose. He at least had no doubt what the end would be, although he fought a losing battle in his examination with great skill and gallantry. He shrank from pain, but mercifully the end was swift, and he met it with a smile. The light that had guided him through triumph and tragedy did not dim its brightness at the last.

CANON GEOFFREY WILLIAM HUGO LAMPE

PROFESSOR OF THEOLOGY IN THE UNIVERSITY OF BIRMINGHAM

5 JULY 1959

Scholar Exeter College Oxford. B.A. 1935, M.A. 1940, B.D. and D.D. 1953, M.C. 1945, F.B.A. 1963. Chaplain and Fellow of St. John's College, Oxford 1943–53. Select Preacher University of Oxford 1951–52. Professor of Theology University of Birmingham 1953–60. Select Preacher University of Cambridge 1956. Honorary Canon of Birmingham 1957–60. Ely Professor of Divinity University of Cambridge from 1960. Canon and Librarian of Ely Cathderal from 1960. Fellow of Gonville and Caius College Cambridge from 1960. Proctor in Convocation University of Cambridge from 1966. Regius Professor of Divinity University of Cambridge from 1971.

6

I take as a text this morning those familiar words from the *Benedictine:* "O ye holy and humble men of heart, praise ye the Lord". It is an appropriate text, for this service commemorates one who is a pre-eminent example of those whom that ancient writer described as holy and humble men of heart.

Saints vary greatly in the attractiveness of their characters. As we look through the volumes of the lives of the great heroes of Christian faith we find a good many, especially among the early hermits and the monastic saints, who seem to us very odd indeed, and some who seem not a little inhuman. We also learn once again the rather obvious truth that it is possible for a man to be both holy and repellent. But Thomas More is one of the best beloved of all holy men. He is a thoroughly attractive saint. He is one of the relatively few who have been wholly dedicated to God and at the same time wholly lovable in their personal relationships and in the way in which they went about their work in this world; and thereby he shows how more truly he lived in the spirit of the gospel than some of those who were in the calendar of the saints long before him. A recent writer remarked that in popular estimation More bids fair today to take the place that was occupied a generation or so ago by Francis of Assisi, and I think this is true. For certainly he sums up in his own person the Christian virtues which most of us ordinary people most admire. He is the great example of a Christian layman. He was a humble man in the proper sense, that is, he was a man who knew his own place in the sight of God and who walked consciously in the sight of God, and therefore was not tempted to think of himself more highly than he ought to think.

He was a man who, unlike so many of those saints in the calendar, was a family man, happy in his own home and delightful as a husband and a father. He was a Christian with a Christian sense of humour, and he was a man possessed of a keen critical mind. An able lawyer and a man of the Renaissance, he was at the same time a devout believer. He was one who saw truth and beauty both in the teaching of the ancient philosophers and in the words of the Christian saints. He was one who believed that reason and faith are never ultimately contradictory to each other.

I think we can claim that Thomas More represents a kind of religion which is peculiarly congenial, and has always been particularly congenial, to Christians in this country. There is a blending in his character of those virtues which we love as a nation to try to cultivate and those which belong particularly and pre-eminently to the Christian as such. He is a great example, perhaps one of the supreme examples, of the English Christian layman. The reasonableness and the sobriety and the beauty of his faith must seem to all of us to be very closely associated not only with those moral characteristics which we most admire in daily life, but also with so much that belongs to the history of our religion in this land: something that harmonises extremely well with the arts and architecture, for instance, of English Christianity; something which is reflected in that combination of moderation and commonsense with piety which is expressed in our liturgy and in the architecture of our churches.

Thomas More may well remind us of that great description which was given long ago, even before the Christian era, by the writer of Ecclesiasticus, of the truly pious man as one who walks humbly before God, who resorts early to his maker and makes confession of his sins, who because of a life grounded in penitence and humility is able to mix with all kinds of people, to travel widely, to read widely, and to adore the best in human learning and culture. More was all of this; and he is, finally, a supreme example of honesty and goodness, of an ethical religion which can stand up to that severest of all tests, the criterion "by their fruits ye shall know them".

Yet I want us this morning to go beyond reflection on his great virtues and to consider the great tragedy of his life. I do not now mean the tragedy of the conflict of loyalty in More's mind between his sovereign and his God. I mean the tragedy of More's bitter conflict with another noble Christian Englishman who, like himself, was to die a martyr's death only exactly a year and a quarter later, on 6 October 1536, and who was to die that martyr's death as the consequence of the successful completion of a hunt which had been instigated by More himself when he visited Antwerp with Tunstall in 1529—a conflict, a tragic conflict, between Thomas More, the Christian humanist, and William Tyndale, one of the chief architects of the English Reformation, to whom we owe the English Bible and in large measure even the actual hallowed and familiar words which have come down to us through successive translations and have finally been enshrined in the Authorised Version.

Here, then, we have a spectacle which is truly tragic, for it is a spectacle of a conflict between two people who were both, according to their lights, in the right. Two people who were motivated by the highest possible principles, two people who were sincerely and honestly devoted to the cause of Christ: Tyndale the priest and More the layman, two Christian men, both devout and holy men, two men who both became martyrs for their faith, and yet two men of whom the one, Tyndale, saw fit to assert of the other, More, that "covetousness blindeth the eyes of that leering fox and hardens his heart against the truth", who was prepared to describe More as a poisonous spider who "spread a dark stinking mist of devilish glosses on the clear text of the scriptures", while the other, More, returned the compliment by calling Tyndale "that beast and hellhound of the devil's kennel".

Of course, we must not be surprised at the vigour of the language used by these two gentlemen of the sixteenth century, for controversial language in that age was apt to be outspoken; but here we have the first great controversy in the English tongue about the doctrine and practice of the medieval church, and it was a controversy which was carried on at immense length over a long period of time. It began with More's very long and very difficult work that is written in an extraordinarily twisted and obscure English style, his work which was called "A Dialogue concerning Heresies and Matters of Religion", written in 1528. It is cast in dialogue form. More pictures himself as sitting in his garden here in Chelsea and receiving a messenger who asks him questions about the new doctrines (they are in fact the doctrines of Tyndale and of Luther) and seeks his opinion and advice about them; and More replies by refuting them. After that long dialogue the controversy was carried on in Tyndale's answer to More's Dialogue, and finally in one of More's last works, written after he had resigned the Chancellorship, his confutation of Tyndale's answer. So the controversy goes on at enormous length and hundreds of thousands of words are spent on it.

As we look back at it now, we may be surprised, not at the vigour and violence of the language which these two great men used towards each other, but rather at their complete failure to understand each other's point of view. They started with a certain amount of agreement; both Tyndale and More were agreed on the pressing need for reformation of some of the obvious administrative and other abuses in the medieval church. On that there were no two opinions; they were both in agreement. Secondly, they were agreed on the need for a vernacular Bible. Many of More's school of thought were afraid to place the English Bible indiscriminately in the hands of the people. But More discounted the fears of many of the clergy; as he says in his Dialogue, "For else if the abuse of the good thing should cause the taking away thereof from another that would use it well, Christ should Himself have never been born". Tyndale's great object, the popularisation of the Bible in the English tongue, was not something with which More himself would necessarily disagree. Thirdly, a point which is often forgotten because so many writers on this subject distort the truth, they were both agreed in

47

their disapproval of King Henry VIII's marriage policy—Tyndale the Reformer as well as More the Catholic.

But More had certain fears which he could not overcome. He was afraid, first of all, that the Reformers' doctrines would be likely to subvert and destroy the authority and the unity of the Church, and authority and unity are two of the primary objects which More kept before himself in all his thinking. Secondly, he thought that the Reformation teachings were likely to replace order by chaos. In a letter to Erasmus, written in 1533, he says: "I so entirely detest that race of men" (he means the Protestants) "that there is none to which I would be more hostile unless they amend. For every day more and more I find them to be of such a sort that I greatly fear for what they are bringing on the world". More evidently had a certain presentiment, well justified by the event, of the dissolution of Christendom that was already beginning.

Thirdly, he thought that these doctrines were likely to subvert ethical religion by antinomianism. We hear a certain amount today from some quarters about the possibility of morality without religion, but it is fortunately characteristic of the English religious tradition that we have an even greater distrust of religion without morality. And More was afraid that the Protestant doctrines would bring precisely that: religion without morality. As he says in his Dialogue against Tyndale: "This they call the liberty of the Gospel, to be discharged of all order and of all laws, and to do what they list, which, be it good or bad, be as they say nothing but the works of God wrought in them. But they hope by this means God shall for the while work in their many merry pastimes. Wherein if their heresy were once received and the world changed thereby, they should find themselves sore deceived. For the laws and orders among men with fear of punishment once taken away, there were no man so strong that could keep his pleasure long, but that he should find a stronger take it from him. But after that it were once come to that point and the world once ruffled and fallen into wildness, how long would it be and what heaps of heavy mischief would there fall, ere the way were found to set the world in order and peace again?" Order and peace, once again, are the chief objects of all More's thought: order and peace which he thought were likely to be subverted by antinomian people who claimed to do what they liked in the name of God.

Now we can see as we look back that More's hope of what is sometimes called an Erasmian Reformation was far too superficial and optimistic. An Erasmian Reformation really amounted to little more in the end than the idea that if only men would cultivate true scholarship, and if only they would cultivate the moderation and the discretion proper to scholars, then surely order and peace could be permanently and securely established. We know in the twentieth century, at least as well as those men in the sixteenth, that the hope that by learning and education alone the really deep and vital problems of the world can be solved is altogether over-optimistic.

So it proved at that time. But there were certain insights which More, for all the beauty of his Christian life and all his zeal for order and unity, could not perceive. There were three vital points on which his controversy with Tyndale was conducted and on which he showed himself totally unable to comprehend what his opponent was thinking and saying. They were, to put it briefly, these.

First, the Reformers saw that the basis of the Christian religion is the saving truth that God accepts sinners. That was what the great controversy about faith and works was ultimately about in the sixteenth century: that God accepts sinners as sinners; that God does not wait for them to become reformed characters, or even wait to make them into reformed characters, before he enfolds them in the arms of His mercy, but that he is like the father in the parable when the son was seen far off down the road coming home: God takes the initiative and runs to meet him. And that was a point which More was really unable to perceive; or at least he was unable to perceive that that was the fundamental point which Luther and Tyndale were making. He was unable to perceive it because in the end he believed that man has to earn the favour of God by doing meritorious works. And when that doctrine was controverted, and the Reformers said in effect: "No. Works are a by-product of a relationship with God which is given solely by grace, solely by God's favour; you do good works because God has already been merciful to you; you don't do good works in order to propitiate God", More, like so many others of his time, failing to understand that point, thought that what the Reformers were saying was: "So long as you have faith it does not matter how you live". Nothing could have been further from their thoughts; but that was the dreadful and tragic misunderstanding which separated these two great Christians in the first place.

The second point was the vital question of scripture and tradition. Today we have to put that problem in rather different terms. But the main issue is still today what it was then: is the faith and practice of the Christian Church ultimately determined by what we have in scripture, or is there another source of authority parallel to scripture, consisting of unwritten tradition, which can demand from us the acceptance of doctrines and practices which the primitive Church knew nothing about? It is a problem with which we are presented in an acute form in this century, since the promulgation of new dogmas by the Church of Rome. Does tradition, unwritten tradition, rank as a separate authority co-ordinate with scripture, or is tradition, in the last resort, subordinate to scripture as its norm? Does scripture in the end control the rest of the tradition? This was the second great problem on which they were divided.

The third was that More, with his love of order and unity, insisted on the absolute inerrancy of the Church. The Church, he said, "can never err in any substantial point that God would have us bounden to believe". God, according to that view, gives a certain and absolute inerrancy to the ecclesistical hierarchy. On the other side, Tyndale believed that God's Spirit does indeed guide the Church into all the truth, but does this by leading and inspiring all those who at any point in time are willing to respond to the Spirit's guidance. Those who are willing to listen to the word of God's Spirit will be guided; and in all ages God raises up faithful men and women who do listen to the Spirit's guidance and become instructors and reformers of the Church. Is the guidance of God's Spirit something which can be channelled into an hierarchical tradition, or is it something which blows where it lists and for which man has always to be on the watch, to listen and to catch that voice of the Spirit? That was the third great issue between them, and those were the great problems which divided Christendom in the sixteenth century and which still divide it today.

As we look back today at the devoted loyalty that both these men gave to the truth as they understood it, we see that for us the problem is how to regain the unity which was then shattered. The unity which More prized so highly was shattered by the insistence of Tyndale and the other Reformers that at all costs, even at the cost of unity, the truth of the gospel must be maintained and preserved. How are we now to get back to that unity? Perhaps there are two ways in which all of us can help.

The first is that we should try more often to recognise the underlying unity which binds together all those who devote themselves to the service of Christ: the underlying unity which subsists at a deeper level than that of theological formulas, the underlying unity which makes both More and Tyndale great Christians and Christian martyrs, the underlying unity which we can see in the inspiration which kept them steadfast to death. We must seek to cultivate that unity, to recognise it wherever we find it. Our Church committed itself in its formulas to the opposite side from More's in that great controversy; but we meet here today to do honour to More, and to wish that those parts of Christendom which adhered to More's doctrine would similarly gather together to do honour to Tyndale. For we recognise that here are two men, both inspired by the one Spirit of God.

Secondly, we can perhaps help by doing more to subordinate our theological disagreements to unity in the service of Christ, practical co-

50

operation in Christian work in an age so largely dominated by utterly non-Christian and materialistic values. Here surely is the call to all Christians to work together in our common allegiance, not first demanding that each one shall subscribe to the same creed, not all demanding that each one shall seek the truth of the gospel in precisely the same terms, but being ready to work together with our fellow Christians in the spirit which inspired those two great men of old, which is the Spirit of Christ Himself.

PROFESSOR CLIFFORD WILLIAM DUGMORE

PROFESSOR OF ECCLESIASTICAL HISTORY
UNIVERSITY OF LONDON

3 JULY 1960

Exeter College Oxford, B.A. 1932, M.A. 1935, B.D. 1940, D.D. 1957. Queen's College Cambridge, B.A.: 1933, M.A. 1936. Senior Lecturer (Ecclesiastical History) University of Manchester 1946–58. Select Preacher University of Cambridge 1956. Professor of Ecclesiastical History University of London 1958–76. F.K.C. 1965. Hulsean Lecturer University of Cambridge 1958–1960. F. R. Hist.S. 1970. Editor of the Journal of Ecclesiastical History since 1950. Member of the Editorial Board of Novum Testamentum since 1956.

Robert Bolt's play *A Man for All Seasons* was first performed at the Globe Theatre, London on 1 JULY 1960. The part of Sir Thomas More was played by Paul Scofield.

52

7

THE twelfth chapter of St. Mark's Gospel, verses 28 and 29: " 'What commandment is the first of all?' Jesus answered: 'Thou shalt love the Lord thy God, with all thy heart and with all thy soul and with all thy mind and with all thy strength. The second is this: Thou shalt love thy neighbour as thyself.' "

Our Lord thus deftly summed up the whole of religion in answer to the question of the Jewish scribes. His answer was taken from Deuteronomy, chapter 6, the Jewish *Shema,* the nearest thing they have to a creed, ("Hear, O Israel"), which was recited daily by every Jew and which Our Lord knew very well was written on the miniature roll which the scribe carried in his phylactery. If you look up Deuteronomy 6, verse 5, you will find no mention of the "mind". The passage runs: "with all thine heart and with all thy soul and with all thy strength". The great Old Testament scholar Dr. Driver pointed out years ago that "in the psychology of the ancient Hebrews" the heart was the organ of intellect, just as the "soul" was the organ of the desires and affections, so that these two embraced "the devotion of the whole being to God".

By the time the Gospels were written, however, the influence of Greek thought and Greek psychology had made itself felt in Palestine and all over the Mediterranean world. The Gospels quote the Old Testament from the Greek Septuagint version. And so we get in Matthew and in Mark the familiar doublets, "with all thy heart and with all thy soul, and with all thy *mind,*" because for the Greeks the heart was not the seat of the intellect as it was for the more primitive Hebrews.

Today our thoughts are particularly directed to the life and work of one who was able to read his New Testament in the original Greek, as a result of the labours of his great friend Erasmus, and I think there can be no doubt that Sir Thomas More, reader at Lincoln's Inn, Under Sheriff of the City of London, Ambassador, Under Treasurer of the Exchequer, Speaker of the House of Commons, High Steward of the Universities of Oxford and of Cambridge, Chancellor of the Duchy of Lancaster and finally Lord Chancellor of England, loved God throughout his life with all his heart and soul and strength, and perhaps above all else with his mind. Born in Cripplegate on the 6th February, 1478, he was "brought up in the Latin tongue at St. Anthony's in London", according to the *Life* written by his son-in-law, William Roper. And even while he was studying law at Lincoln's Inn he began to study Greek with Grocyn the vicar of St. Lawrence, Jewry, and then with Linacre, about the turn of the century. A first class scholar, something of a saint, a man of peace, but also a man of principle, he regularly worshipped in this church after he moved to Chelsea from the City. And he was beheaded on St. Thomas's eve, the 6th July, 1535, within the octave of St. Peter, for conscience sake, because as he told Lord Chancellor Audley at his trial, his indictment for high treason was "grounded on an Act of Parliament directly repugnant to the laws of God and His holy church . . . and therefore am I not bound, My Lord, to conform my conscience to the Council of one realm against the general council of Christendom".

In the programme note on his remarkably fine portrayal of More in his play *A Man for All Seasons* which is now running at the Globe Theatre, Robert Bolt writes: "He was a pivot of English life at a time when England was negotiating the sharpest corner in her spiritual history." If Paul Scofield shows us More in the role of a witty but somewhat absent-minded professor, completely dedicated to the thought of martyrdom and apparently insensible to his duty to and responsibility for his wife and family, we have to remember that no single play, any more than a single sermon, can give a complete picture of so gifted and so great a man. Moreover, like most of us, he had a highly complex personality.

If we want to see what dedication to duty as he understood it really cost him, we must read his *Dialogue of Comfort against Tribulations,* his *Treaties on the Passion,* his *Treaties to Receive the Blessed Body of Our Lord* and his *Certain Devout Meditations,* all written while he was a prisoner in the tower in 1534–5. His English works were gathered together in 1557 and published, by command of Queen Mary, under the editorship of More's nephew, Justice William Rastell, the elder son of the printer, John Rastell. He included a collection of prayers, one of which we heard a few moments ago, and these prayers give us I think an insight into his love for God, with all his heart and soul and mind: "Good Lord, give me the grace, in all my fear and agony, to have recourse to that great fear and wonderful agony that Thou, my sweet Saviour, hadst at the Mount of Olivet before Thy most bitter passion, and in the meditation thereof to conceive ghostly comfort and consolation profitable for my soul. . . . Almighty God, have mercy on N. and N. and on all that bear me evil will . . . Lord, give me patience in tribulation and grace in everything to conform my will to Thine, that I may truly say—fiat voluntas tua, sicut in caelo et in terra. Amen."

There is the true saint. The language is a far cry from that of the brilliant young scholar who wrote probably for the Sergeants' Feast of

1503, when his father, John More, was one of the newly elected Sergeants at Arms, lines which could easily have come from a Gilbert and Sullivan opera: "When a hatter will go smatter in philosophy, or a pedlar wax a meddler in theology, no good will come of it". "Already", says Professor Chambers, from whom I cite these lines, "More recognised the danger of the busy meddler in theology". Thus, he argued long and earnestly against his son-in-law Roper, when that young man for a time adopted the Lutheran belief in justification by faith alone, and finally he told his daughter, Margaret, that he could only resort to prayer. Strangely enough, Roper was subsequently converted to orthodoxy.

More wrote learned treatises against Tyndale and against John Frith's teaching on the sacrament, declaring that the latter "wyll for the allegorye destroye the trewe sense of the letter, in mayntenance of a newe false secte, agaynste the hole trewe catholyke fayth so fully confyrmed and contynued in Christes whole Catholyke · Churche, thys XV.C yere togyder". And yet, More was no diehard obscurantist. Although he upheld the Old Religion he was a son of the renaissance. A friend of Grocyn, Collet and Fisher—he entertained both Erasmus and Andrew Ammonio here in his house in Chelsea. As Speaker of the House of Commons, he stood for free speech in parliament and he refused to be browbeaten by Wolsey. He favoured the translation of the scriptures into English—but not that they might be argued about in taverns and made, as he says, "the subject for every lewd lad to keep a pot parliament upon". His *Utopia,* of course, is a classic of the English language.

I remarked earlier that More was a scholar and a saint, but also, supremely, a man of peace and a man of principle. He was utterly opposed to Wolsey's foreign policy. War was to him the great enemy of learning and of true religion. William Roper tells us that: "on a time, walking with me along the Thames side at Chelsea, and talking of other things, he said unto me: 'Now would to Our Lord, son Roper, upon condition that three things were well established in Christendom, I were put in a sack, and here presently cast into the Thames'. 'What great things be those, sir' quoth I . . . 'In faith, son, they be these,' said he. 'The first is that where the most part of Christian princes be at mortal war, they were all at an universal peace'." The second and third were the settlement of heresy and the conclusion of the King's matter of his marriage. But the order of the three is noteworthy. Peace first. So too is the fact that the only public event mentioned by More in the epitaph which he wrote for his tomb. which stands against the south wall in the sanctuary of this church, is the peace which was signed with France at Cambrai in 1529. He never quarrelled with Wolsey nor with his master the King. The Cardinal went out with the famous words recorded by his usher, George Cavendish, who incidentally married a niece of Thomas

More, "If I had served God half as diligently as I have done the King, He would not have given me over in my grey hairs." More put things the other way round. He was "the King's servant, but God's first". He recognised the King's need for an heir, and the right of the King in parliament to fix the succession but further than that he would not go. More had always been the champion of Katherine of Aragon. At last, on the 23rd May 1533, the King's business was brought to a close: Cranmer pronounced that the marriage of Henry and Katharine was null and void. Five days later he declared that the marriage of Henry and Anne Boleyn was valid, and on 1st June 1533 Anne was crowned in the Abbey. More refused to attend the coronation, although his Catholic friends Tunstall, Clerk and Gardiner went. And this action cost him his life, because Anne never forgave him.

If Master Thomas Cromwell, to use theological language, was the instrumental cause of his death, Anne Boleyn was the proximate cause. According to Cresacre More, "when news of his death was brought to the King, who was at that time playing at tables, Anne Boleyn looking on, he cast his eye upon her and said: 'thou art the cause of this man's death,' and presently leaving his play he betook himself unto his chamber, and thereupon fell into a fit of melancholy".

We may sympathise with More, or we may sympathise with Anne. One thing is clear. The charge that the Reformation in England was entirely due to Henry's lust for Anne which is still perpetuated by some Roman Catholic historians, is historically absurd and is grounded upon Victorian morality. If Henry had not been King of England the Pope would never have granted him a dispensation to marry Katharine at all. If he had not been at the mercy of the Emperor Charles he would have granted him the divorce which Cranmer granted. An heir to the throne was imperative if England was not to experience a "War of the Roses" again. More himself admitted that, but he steadfastly refused to take the oath which amounted to a final repudiation of the papal authority. The tragedy of his death lies in the fact that he belonged half to mediaeval England and half to modern England. He lived at the end of an era and so, as Mr. Bolt has said, "he became a martyr against his desires".

Yes, but is that really true? All his life More put God first and, according to his lights, he loved God with all his heart and soul and mind and strength. As a young man studying law at Lincoln's Inn he lived for about four years at the Charterhouse, sharing the religious life of the monks, though not living under vow. Erasmus tells us that he nearly became a priest, but could not abandon his desire for the wedded state. In fact, within a month of the death of his first wife he married a second wife, Dame Alice, whom he described as "neither a pearl nor a girl". All his life

More wore a hair shirt next to his skin, which his daughter Margaret used to wash. At heart he was a son of the mediaeval church, firmly believing in purgatory and the merit of good works. This is clear, I think, from a passage in his talk with Margaret Roper during his imprisonment in the Tower: "I cannot, I say, therefore distrust the grace of God, but that either He shall conserve me and keep the King in that gracious mind still to do to me none hurt, or else, if his pleasure be, that for mine other sins I shall suffer in such a case in sight as I shall not deserve, his grace shall give me the strength to take it patiently, and peradventure somewhat gladly too, whereby his high goodness shall (by the merits of his bitter passion joined thereunto, and far surpassing in merit for me all that I can suffer myself) make it serve for release of my pain in purgatory, and over that for increase of some reward in heaven". Frequently he speaks in his letters from the Tower of meeting his family and friends together in heaven, "where we shall make merry for ever and never have trouble after". He was a son of the mediaeval church.

This was his way of putting God first. There were others in his age who also loved God with all their heart and soul and strength and mind, in different ways, but no less sincerely, and often unto death. There were Frith and Tyndale, and later there were Cranmer and Ridley, as well as Latimer and Fisher, and a multitude which cannot be numbered on both sides of the gulf which developed between reformed and unreformed. The peace for which More longed had departed, but the church was born anew.

There is no longer an hour glass in this pulpit, as no doubt there was when it was a three-decker before 1908, but the sand is running out. I will end by passing on to you a thought expressed by the writer of the book *Erasmus, Tyndale and More*. W. E. Campbell quotes from More's *Dialogue concerning Tyndale* this passage: "Every man, as Aesop saith in a fable, carrieth a double wallet on his shoulder: and into the one that hangeth at his breast he putteth other folks' faults and therein he looketh and poreth often. In the other, he layeth all his own, and swingeth it at his back, which himself never listeth to look in, but other that come after him cast an eye in among". "And does it not seem" says Campbell, "from this simple spiritual truth, that the way to become better oneself consists in turning the wallets round, so that we have our own faults under our own gaze, and those of other people well behind us, though God may wish us to carry them nevertheless".

We are not all called to be martyrs like Thomas More, but perhaps this is one way in which we ordinary Christians can learn to love God with all our heart, soul, mind, and strength, just a little better perhaps than we do at present, *and* our neighbour as ourself.

THE VERY REVEREND ROBERT LESLIE POLLINGTON MILBURN

DEAN OF WORCESTER

2 JULY 1961

Scholar Sidney Sussex College, Cambridge
B.A. 1930, M.A. 1934, New College Oxford
1933. Fellow and Chaplain Worcester College
Oxford 1934–57. Select Preacher University
of Oxford 1942–44. University Lecturer in
Church History 1947–59. Bampton Lecturer
1952. Dean of Worcester 1957–68. Select
Preacher University of Cambridge 1963.
Master of the Temple from 1968.

8

THE fifteenth chapter of St. John's Gospel and the twenty-sixth verse: "The Comforter whom I will send unto you from the Father even the spirit of truth".

There are in the course of history long ages without a name, when the current events of thought flow sluggishly and the energies of mankind seem to be taken up almost entirely with the routine business of living. But the spirit bloweth where it listeth and so from time to time a strange upsurge of power and insight may visit a nation. And then the ordinary, competitive round pales in importance before some new and rich discovery—some keener awareness it may be of God and of the works which manifest His truth.

And so five centuries before the coming of Christ in violet-crowned Athens, a city no larger than Chelsea, and harassed by continual warfare, the poets, the architects, the law-givers, suddenly arise whose genius, mingling with that of the people of the Hebrews, has produced the form and the pattern of our civilization.

The spirit may not remain long. A century went by and Athens sank to the level of a quiet provincial capital. But in other places and in other ages the spirit God in action bursts forth vigorously as once in the Creation of the World so now in the hearts of men whom God appoints as His agents to control its destinies.

The Twelve Apostles and their friends appointed by Christ to be the pillars of His new Israel were promised an especial gift of power "when the Holy Ghost is come upon you" in order that they might bring new confidence to a world from which hope had fled and be His witnesses unto the uttermost parts of the earth. But the long history of the Christian Church displays, together with much eager devotion, periods of bitter warfare and gloomy stagnation.

One such was the close of the Middle Ages: from which Europe suddenly revived in a burst of tumultuous and many-sided activity—a burst which goes under the name of the Renaissance: the rebirth of free enquiry and surprising discovery in all fields. It was of course in the close-packed cities of Italy, Florence or Rome or Bologna, where this new spirit of eager questioning found clearest expression, whether in the arts of painting and architecture, or in bold attempts at politics, the science which teaches the difficult lesson how man should live in harmony with his neighbour. But, about the time that Henry VII was giving place to his son, England also was not without its group of enlightened scholars and diligent law-givers who almost seemed, like Moses of old, to stand apart from the common run of mankind and speak face to face with the living God.

One such—it might reasonably be claimed—was Thomas More. Fortunate alike in his natural ability and in his upbringing, More enjoyed his days at school and at Oxford where his tutors were men of fresh and eager mind and his circumstances so restricted that, we read, he had no opportunity to neglect his studies for frivolous amusements.

More's father was afraid that Thomas's enthusiasm for the New Learning, based on the long forgotten wisdom of the Greeks, might unsettle his faith in the teachings of the Church. But in fact More found nothing dangerous in pagan speculations. "He that is not against me is with Me" he repeated as he thumbed the Gospels. And he attacked those "Barbarians" as he called them at Oxford who refused to extend the boundaries of learning beyond the limits which had satisfied the Church-men of the Middle Ages. In all this he was following the line of St. Justin, a second-century convert to Christianity who was no lukewarm believer but met death for his faith with a calm and gentlemanly determination. This St. Justin lays it down that "whatsoever has been nobly said or nobly done by anybody anywhere belongs to us Christians." And what he seems to mean by this remark is that, just as there is but one Lord of history who according to the Prophets brings the Philistines from Caphtor and the Syrians from Kiz as well as Israel out of the land of Egypt, so there is but one Lord of Life from whom proceed goodness and beauty and to whose inspiration whatever is fair and of good report must be assigned. "Time always tryeth out the truth", so More put it, and he added that reason, so far from being an enemy to faith, is servant to faith.

More was well aware of the corruptions which marked the Church of his day. But like his friend Colet, the founder of St. Paul's School, he hoped for a quiet Reformation from within as men became better educated and he had no sympathy with Luther's more drastic methods. Intelligent, peace-loving, quietly conservative, he desired the welfare of all and was sufficiently clear-sighted to see that this aim would not be secured by a revolution. In any government, he realised, in any church, there will be found, so long as human nature lasts, some element of weakness and imperfection. It is not possible—this is how More puts it—"it is not possible for all things to be well unless all men were good which I think will not be yet these many years".

Brilliant success at the Bar was followed for More by a graceful period when he enjoyed the exceptional favour of Henry VIII and was entrusted with a wide variety of delicate commissions at home and abroad. The new-found love of learning had touched the King closely and in his private rooms he would talk with More, so it is recorded, of astronomy, geometry, divinity and "such other faculties". Sometimes King Henry would pay a call on More and stroll about More's garden in Chelsea, placing his arm about his counsellor's neck. More, however, was not the kind of person to be deceived by flattering attentions. "If my head should ever win a castle in France," he said to a friend, "I should not fail to lose it."

But that was in 1525 when More, as Speaker of the House of Commons, had already shown a certain stiffness in his treatment of Cardinal Wolsey. But this time he was feeling the weight of high political office, whereas earlier he had drawn unalloyed happiness from his travels as an ambassador to France and the Low Countries. Whilst at Antwerp in 1516 he composed the first draft of his fantasy *Utopia*—the only example of his literary work which is likely to survive. "Utopia"—the word means a place nowhere to be found, even though More describes a traveller visiting it—this *Utopia,* for all its touches of irony, clearly reveals More's humane and generous outlook just as it offers hints, sometimes courageous hints to King and priest alike. There is for instance a protest against the great and horrible punishments appointed for thieves, "whereas much rather", as More puts it, "provision should be made that there might be some means whereby they could get their living." More was a devoted churchman, yet in his zeal for social justice he had no hesitation in alluding to certain Abbots, holy men no doubt, "who do not content themselves with their yearly revenues and profits but leave no ground for tillage, throw down houses, pluck down towns and leave nothing standing but only the Church to be a sheep house."

Again, in Tudor times, it was bold for a courtier even though half in jest to refer to the monarchy as "a device whereby one man may live in pleasure and wealth while all others weep and smart for it." "This," added More, "is the part not of a king but of a gaoler". Moreover warfare—at one time the sport of kings—is condemned as a thing very beastly and yet to no kind of beasts in so much use as to man. The Utopians, so it was reported, train both men and women in the use of arms but never go to battle save in defence of their own country or "to deliver from the yoke and bondage of tyranny some people that are therewith oppressed."

As regards family life, Thomas More, like the people of Utopia, chose that sober, genial fashion which recalls to the minds of some the ways of the Old Testament patriarchs—Abraham, Isaac and the rest—

61

and which was later reproduced in many a country vicarage in the Victorian Age. The scholar Erasmus, who had walked along the bank of the Thames to visit More was most impressed. "Plato's Academy," he wrote, "is revived again. Only, whereas in the Academy the discussions turned on geometry and the power of number, the house at Chelsea is a veritable school of the Christian religion. In it is no one, man or woman, who does not read or study the liberal arts, yet is their chief care of piety. No one is ever idle. The head of the house governs it not by lofty carriage and frequent rebukes but by gentleness and amiable manners. Every member is busy in his place performing his duty with alacrity nor is sober mirth wanting." To this description the picture which Holbein painted of the More family bears witness. The little monkey, chained but contented, that hops about near Lady More illustrates their fondness on which many remarked for animals and birds. More was by this time Lord High Chancellor of England, performing his duties with an admirable and gracious competence yet continually vexed by the King's determination to divorce Katharine of Aragon in favour of Ann Boleyn. He was also being drawn into quarrels about religion which brought a harsh note into the tolerant happy life of this Renaissance scholar and man of affairs. In Utopia the people agree together that there is one chief and principal God, the maker and ruler of the whole world, and then the writer goes on to explain: "They think that the contemplation of nature and the praise thereof is to God a very acceptable honour." It is almost as though More were anticipating the faith of a poet of our day—"I love all beauteous things, I seek and adore them, God hath no better praise and man in his hasty days is honoured for them." Those who dwell in Utopia gladly received the Christian religion when it was preached to them. They saw in it the natural culmination of God's message, His word, which, spelt out letter by letter in the inspired utterance of poet, priest or prophet, receives its final expression in the unmistakable and international language of human life.

Nevertheless in true Renaissance fashion, these Utopians were concerned rather to proclaim and live by the truth than to oppress those whose religious awareness was less perfect than their own. And the story is told of how one Christian convert in Utopia was sharply punished because "he began to wax so hot in his matter that he did utterly despise and condemn all other religions, calling them profane and their followers wicked and devilish." And this unfortunately is just the kind of language which was being used in More's day; not between Christians and others, but between Christians of two opposing factions, as the power of Rome was challenged by an explosion of vigour concerned less with papal decrees than with the Scriptures and the practices of the primitive Church. More's own tastes were largely in agreement with such an approach. He liked forms of worship that were simple and direct and he annoyed the Duke of Norfolk, who thought him foolish for putting on a surplice and singing heartily in the choir of this church.

Yet his high office and the circumstances of the day drew More into bitter argument on the other side. When Luther attacked Henry VIII he defended his Royal Master in what he called "a bantering rejoinder" but the tone of his pamphlets was gradually sharpened on the anvil of controversy. Strangely enough his most savage attacks were directed against William Tyndale, another seeker after truth whose aim was to make the Scriptures available in the English language and whose work underlies all our versions of the Bible. "Neither doth he abhor anything that is evil"— the Psalmist text sums up a real fruit in a man's character. And More may well have had this in mind when he made onslaughts on persons whom he regarded as dangerously in error. His tomb used to bear the words, removed in 1833 as "unedifying", Haereticis Molestus: the sworn foe of all heretics. And the excitement of religious controversy sometimes caused More to forget the urbane teachings of the Renaissance scholars, with their desire to find good in all men and some touch of the Spirit of God in all religion.

When John Tewkesbury, a poor leather seller, was burnt in December 1531, More observed "there never was a wretch I wean better worthy such a death". He had perhaps for the moment forgotten that those who take the sword may perish by the sword. Yet the manner of his own passing was noble enough.

Controversies of a past age, so vital at the time, are as one looks back on them apt to appear tragic or even ridiculous. The argument between Henry VIII and More revolved round the title "Supreme Head of the Church of England" as applied to the King. More imagined that the words assigned to Henry a spiritual power to propound church doctrine, whereas for Henry the importance of the title was political—"there can be but one fountain head of Law in the country". Deaf to the laments of his distracted family, More refused to yield on a matter which he claimed to have studied for seven years. And when, with an almost carefree gaiety, he laid his head upon the block, he bore witness to this: that man's life on earth is not merely a thing of shreds and patches but that enriched and dignified by the Spirit of God it may be used, and surrendered, in the service of truth.

THE REVEREND DAVID LAWRENCE EDWARDS

EDITOR OF THE STUDENT CHRISTIAN MOVEMENT PRESS

1 JULY 1962

Demy of Magdalen College Oxford, B.A. 1952, M.A. 1956. Fellow of All Souls College, Oxford 1952–59. Tutor Westcott House Cambridge 1954–55. Editor of the Student Christian Movement Press 1959–66. Select Preacher University of Cambridge 1960, Oxford 1972 and 1974. Fellow and Dean of Kings College Cambridge 1966–70. Hulsean Lecturer University of Cambridge 1966–68. Divinity Lecturer from 1967. Canon of Westminster and Rector of St. Margaret's, Westminster from 1970. Sub-Dean from 1974. Speaker's Chaplain from 1972.

9

I take as my text some words from the Old Testament which occur just before the First Lesson read to us this morning. I Kings, 8: 30—*Hear thou in Heaven thy dwelling place, and when thou hearest forgive.*

This is the prayer of King Solomon at the dedication of the Temple in Jerusalem. And it acknowledges that God does not dwell in this temple in the sense of being confined to it. The same theme is taken up in the New Testament. Always true religion, pure religion, must confess that the eternal God is greater than any religious institution. No Church can imprison God. No Church can monopolise God. No Church can understand the full truth about God. God does not even live in the sky, although He is sometimes pictured there. He lives everywhere; he is present throughout all that exists and He lives also beyond what exists. God minus the world—as Archbishop William Temple used to say—God minus the world equals God. This is what we really affirm when we say that Heaven is God's home, and because we know that God is so great our prayer to Him must be that He will be patient with our littleness.

Yet we need places which help us to make this prayer to the eternal God and these places are the temples and the churches which we have built. So Solomon while he says *Behold heaven cannot contain thee, how much less this house,* goes on to ask that God's *ears may be open night and day towards this house, that thou mayest hearken to the prayer which thy servant offers.* And so the New Testament, while teaching that God is greater than any institution, teaches also that we need the Church, the institutional Church, the organised Church, the fellowship of disciples with its Scriptures and its sacraments. The New Testament indeed teaches us to love the Church because the Church is the place or the fellowship where it is easiest to communicate with God. Here we may know that the mysterious God is also a merciful God who delights to speak with us as a man speaks with his friend.

What has that to do with Sir Thomas More? Solomon and Sir Thomas More were separated from each other by two and a half thousand years, and we are separated by four hundred years from Sir Thomas More. But we can recognise in King Solomon and in Sir Thomas More certain characteristics which we can admire today. These men were men of culture and men of power. Solomon in all his glory was the worldly

65

climax of the history of Israel, his wisdom and his wealth became legendary. Sir Thomas More was steeped in much of the learning and the intellectual excitement of the Renaissance, his book on Utopia was not only a brilliant literary feat but also a subtle essay in political philosophy, and as a lawyer and politician he rose to the top of his profession, being Chancellor of England.

But Solomon and Sir Thomas More had also this in common: that they believed in God. With all their cleverness and their political prestige they identified themselves with a temple and a church where they sought after God and found Him. And they are remembered today primarily because of the parts they played in the story of the people of God. In Jerusalem and in Chelsea they knew the mysterious God and the merciful God.

I think that we may compare King Solomon and Sir Thomas More in another way also: they were men whose lives seemed to end in tragedy. Their hopes were apparently wrecked by history. And yet history in the long run—or perhaps we'd better say frankly *God,* working in His mysterious ways—has brought to them a fulfilment even on this earth, a fulfilment which is beyond tragedy, an achievement enduring after apparent defeat. The God whom they served did not betray them.

Solomon, as we heard in the First Lesson, boasted that not one word of God's promises had failed. There was a time when God's promises seemed to fail utterly. Solomon's temple was destroyed by the Babylonians and the little kingdom over which he reigned was blotted out. The temple and the nation were restored and then once more blotted out by the Romans. What endured, however, was the essential idea of a people around a temple dedicated to God. That idea you still find in the last Book of the Bible, the Revelation of St. John the Divine with the vision of the new Jerusalem, and the new people of God, when all on earth had failed. That idea is the heart of the Jewish religion and it continues into our time. What matters for us even more is that here is the foundation of the Christian Church. Our temple is invisible because our temple is the work of Jesus Christ and our nation is invisible because it is the Church of all times and all places as the new Israel, the royal priesthood, the holy nation of which our Second Lesson spoke. So in the long run Solomon's prayer at the dedication of the temple was answered.

Looking back on Sir Thomas More's life from the 1960's, we can see that his prayer also is beginning to find fulfilment in the events around us.

Sir Thomas More refused to acknowledge King Henry VIII as Supreme head of the Church of England. He was not a fanatical Roman Catholic; he was a loyal one, but not a fanatical one. He said some very critical things about the Church and about the Papacy. But in the end he preferred his Pope to his King in religious matters. He was executed and apparently his cause was wrecked; his cause as well as his life. For from that day to this the great majority of the English people has rejected the claims of the Popes. No Popery is one of the central themes in our nation's story.

Moreover, within the Roman Catholic Church the bitterness of the struggle with Protestantism has resulted in a centralisation of power and elaboration of doctrine which I think More would have regretted; for More was in Roman Catholic terms definitely a layman and a liberal layman and proud to be so. So apparently More threw his life away; history has brought this firm division between a Protestant England and an increasingly dogmatic and authoritarian Roman Catholic Church. Apparently that is the result.

Yet this is not the whole truth. Today more and more Christians throughout the world are awakening to the two causes which were at the heart of this martyr's attitude. These two causes may be described as Christian integrity and Christian unity. Sir Thomas More defied his King when his King claimed the power to decide religious matters. We must remember that Henry VIII claimed the right to define doctrine and to punish heresy. Sir Thomas More maintained that these religious powers belonged to the Church alone, and that Jesus Christ was the Church's only supreme head. Sir Thomas More was right. And in our own century when many Christians in many countries have been called to stand for the things of God against tyranny we can see that he was right. The State has its own role to play, given to it by God; national government and local government are sacred. Sir Thomas More, Chancellor of England, knew that and we know it. The powers that be are ordained of God. But it is not within the right of the State to override Christian conscience or to interfere with the internal affairs of the Christian Church, with its liberty to be the Christian Church in obedience to its Lord.

More laid down his life gladly to proclaim that truth. So did many Christians who resisted Hitler; Christians in the occupied countries of Europe, Christians within Germany itself. Many of them paid with their lives for their resistance. Other martyrs in exactly the same cause are to be found in the story of Christians under Communism. And in Africa Christians have been called to bear the same witness against racialism when this has been enforced by the State. The black Christians in Kenya who refused to support Mau Mau and who were murdered were martyrs in the struggle against racialism backed by brute force. So too have been the white Christians in South Africa who have refused to compromise with the racialism of the government. And other examples could be given of the price paid by Christians in defying the tyrannies, the plentiful tyrannies, of the twentieth century.

These examples should cause us to think again about the relationship of Church and State in our own country. Does that relationship give proper freedom to the Church to be the Church? This question, raised by the Archbishop of Canterbury among others, is now in the air. I won't go into it now, I will just point out that Sir Thomas More, whom we honour today, is one of the patron saints of Christian integrity and his example must mean more than perhaps any other man's example to English Christians.

And Sir Thomas More stood also for Christian unity. He claimed that England had no right to cut itself off from the rest of the Christian Church. And he was essentially correct. You and I feel that it has been tragically necessary for the Church of England to hold itself apart from the Papacy these four hundred years. For to submit to the Papacy as the Papacy has been would have been to have compromised our Christian integrity. You and I feel that it has been necessary. But that does not make it any less of a tragedy. It has not been right for England to be isolated from other Christian Churches, any more than it has been right for Scotland or for Italy or for Greece. The Christian Church is meant to be one. Not uniform, the Church of the New Testament is not uniform, but one fellowship, one army.

Although in the short run Christian integrity may demand protests and splits and controversies, in the long run Christian integrity must lead to Christian unity. As we agree in obeying our common Lord, Jesus Christ. And in our day many are feeling their way towards Christian unity; many in the Church of England, many in the Protestant Free Churches, many in the Roman Catholic Church, led by the generous hearted Pope John XXIII, many are feeling their way towards this unity, and the Second Vatican Council which is to assemble in Rome this Autumn is to be a great incident in this story. We are seeking to be delivered from all pride and prejudice, seeking unity in the Church such as the Middle Ages knew—only this time it is to be a purer unity. The search is full of difficulty, especially for us in England where divisions are so deep, but the search must go forward and there is Sir Thomas More to encourage us.

It may be therefore that God is on our time, answering those prayers which Sir Thomas More offered when he was a parishioner in this parish church and when he was a prisoner kneeling under the executioner's axe. Or it may be that God will delay for further centuries before He gives us the full spirit of Christian integrity and Christian unity. But we know that God does in His own time answer prayers made to Him by men such as

Thomas More, the knight and saint. Solomon prayed to the eternal God, high and remote in His Majesty and His mystery, he prayed that God would hear and would forgive, would bless the temple in Jerusalem, and in the end after much apparent delay God came in one greater than Solomon, God provided a temple made without hands and God's blessing remained upon His people. Thomas More prayed that his life itself might be accepted as a proclamation of Christian integrity and Christian unity. When he could no longer speak about such things with his learning and his wit, he made his life itself his speech. We cannot doubt that the God who heard King Solomon has heard Sir Thomas More. Mysterious as God is, He is also merciful. He has heard in Heaven, for night and day His ears are open.

THE REVEREND WILLIAM GORDON FALLOWS

PRINCIPAL OF RIPON HALL, OXFORD

7 JULY 1963

St. Edmund Hall, Oxford B.A. 1935, M.A. 1939. Proctor in Convocation Blackburn 1950–55. Chaplain to H.M. the Queen 1954–68. Archdeacon of Lancaster 1955–59. Principal of Ripon Hall, Oxford 1959–68. Select Preacher University of Oxford 1961. Lord Bishop Suffragan of Pontefract 1968–71. Bishop of Sheffield from 1971. Clerk of the Closet to the Queen from 1975.

10

I take as my text for what I want to say to you this morning the verse from the third chapter of St. Paul's Epistle to the Colossians, verse 23: Whatsoever ye do, do it heartily as unto the Lord and not unto men.

In his biography of King George V, Mr. Harold Nicolson tells of how on one occasion when George V was himself a young sailor, he addressed the cadets of the training ship *Conway* and spoke to them of the three qualities required of a sailor: first truthfulness, without which no man can gain the confidence of those below him; secondly, obedience, without which no man can gain the confidence of those above him; thirdly, zest, without which no seaman is worth his salt.

Now it's about this third quality which George V spoke to those cadets of on the training ship *Conway,* about this third quality, zest, without which I would say no Christian is worth his salt, that I want specially to speak to you this morning in this service in which we honour the memory of Sir Thomas More. For this is the quality in his life and character that seems to me most dominant. This zest, and with it a cheerfulness, that was always breaking in, no matter by what disasters or by what sorrows he was momentarily beset. Mental *joie de vivre* that only those who live close to God can know—this for me is the hallmark of the life and character of Sir Thomas More. And he, being dead, yet speaketh, and he speaks to our condition. Indeed, there are so many ways in which the preacher might speak of Sir Thomas More and all of them would be ways which are specially relevant to the spiritual needs of our own time. The preacher might choose to dwell on the home life of Sir Thomas More, and what perhaps more appropriate at the end of Christian Family Year. For surely Thomas More was what I would call a secular saint; you remember how he studied for some three years at the Charterhouse in preparation for a monastic life. He studied for the cloister, but was drawn to the hearth. He repudiates the monastery in favour of matrimony. And we speak, do we not, of the household of Sir Thomas More, not simply because Holbein painted the family group, but surely because it was a household of unusual domestic harmony. The affection of a widowed father after the loss of his first wife for his motherless children, and then the stepmother who comes into the home with such complete success; the son-in-law who was more like a son, the children with their pets who were

71

shown to the distinguished visitors who were ever in and out of the house. Here we have a picture of home life at its best. You can't really know Sir Thomas More until you have stepped across the doorstep into his household. Some men you can know without knowing them at home—Sir Thomas More you can only know when you are admitted into the sanctity of his home life.

Or again the preacher might choose to speak of his integrity: he was the same right through. And is not this a message which comes with relevance to our present needs and to our present times? He died, said Seebohm, a martyr to integrity. The King as you remember often conversed with him in his Chelsea home and More's abilities and the royal favour advanced him to positions of the highest eminence. But he had the courage and the integrity to resign his high office and to meet death cheerfully when his convictions and his conscience dictated such a course. He was a man of independent spirit, a man with a mind of his own. Erasmus tells us of him: "None is less guided by the opinions of the herd, but again none is less remote from the common feeling of humanity". Yet his integrity—if we may use the colloquialism—sticks out a mile and pray God, we shall see it and emulate it.

Or again, the preacher might choose to dwell on More as a satirist and a critic and a reformer. And here again he speaks to our condition. We are witnessing in our own generation a revival of the art of satire, we are forever tilting at the Establishment, pricking bubbles of convention. In the year of "That Was The Week That Was", in the age of "Private Eye", in the era of Theatre Workshop and "Beyond the Fringe" and the like, in all this healthy satiric fun, Sir Thomas More is an exemplar to our age. For he brings to all his work a delicate wit and a fine intellect, but there is never any bitterness in his satire. And malice is a stranger both to his tongue and to his pen.

In More's *Utopia*, as in his Chelsea home, the pleasures of the mind are—and here I quote: "the cheapest and most principal of all". He can use his critical intelligence and his rapier wit to devastating effect; he can condemn evils where he sees evils. Gambling and hunting for instance he describes as unfit for free men. Hunting he calls the lowest, vilest and most abject part of butchery. He has no time for astrology and for the other current superstitions of his day, which he calls the will of the wisp of the medieval intellect. Yet he is essentially a modern man and a Renaissance man. In *Utopia* there is not only a form of euthanasia and a system of universal education, but there are no lawyers. And, (*pace* our Roman Catholic friends by whom the author a few years ago was canonised), in *Utopia* women were priests. But in all these aspects of More as critic and satirist and as reformer, in all this questioning spirit, in all this tilting at hallowed institutions and at established conventions, there is underlying it all, as it seems to me, a faith in reason and a spirit of reverence. And it is this marriage of reason and of reference that saves his work from triviality and redeems it from all bitterness. And it is just here I believe that he speaks to the bubble-prickers and the 'Aunt Sally Shysters' of our own time. Again if I may quote Erasmus, his friend: "From his boyhood he has loved joking", but his joking never descended to buffoonery and he never loved the biting jest.

Yet he speaks to our condition. But appealing as all this aspect of Thomas More is, and relevant as it is and contemporary as it is, I would nevertheless choose to stress what I have called his zest and his cheerfulness—he lived heartily. And that's why I have chosen as our text for our service today those words of St. Paul: And whatsoever ye do, do it heartily as unto the Lord and not unto man. St. Paul is speaking of the new life in Christ: "If ye then be risen with Christ seek those things that are above". And then follows an exhortation to put on a heart of compassion, kindness, humility, meekness, long suffering, forebearing one another and forgiving each other. And let the peace of Christ dwell and rule in your heart. And as always with St. Paul when he is preaching the great themes he soon comes to practical applications. And here he speaks of the practical application of what he is saying in terms of human relationships. First as between husband and wife, then as between parents and children: "Provoke not your child to wrath". Then as between masters and servants. And it is indeed to the servants that the words of my text are addressed: "Whatsoever ye do, do it heartily as unto the Lord and not unto men". Please God with what you are doing and don't really worry about what men think of you. Just have your minds set upon fulfilling the will of God and doing His pleasure. Although in the context the words have a limited reference to the world of slaves of the ancient world surely they are words that apply to us all, and which we might in fact translate: put zest into all you do. If a seaman is not worth his salt without zest so too every Christian is failing in his vocation until he has learned to put zest into all he does. "Whatsoever ye do, do it heartily as unto the Lord".

This little word zest has an interesting history. It isn't in fact itself a New Testament word, by derivation it is a French word and it means originally the peel of an orange or a lemon used in flavouring, and so, figuratively, whatever adds savour to living—and so, if we may so put it, the spice of life. As we think of the little word zest in that way, in reference to its origin, cannot we say of our Lord that Christ is the man of zest. And as we learn from Him, and as we walk with Him, will we not learn to put zest into life, to find for ourselves the spice of life. Now this I believe is the true secret of the life and character of Sir Thomas More.

"What has nature ever fashioned"—writes Erasmus again—"gentler or sweeter or happier than the character of Thomas More". Yet he was one of those Christian souls the very recollection of whom is an inspiration to their friends. And that's indeed what he was. "I used to enjoy," says Erasmus again, "the memory of you in absence, even as I was wont to delight in your present company". What a wonderful thing it is to have that said of anyone, that there is a joy to people when they think about them in their absence, as they are a joy to them when they are present. Doesn't that speak to us and to our needs as well, and doesn't it remind us to thank God for the memory of our friends.

There are those whose very presence breathes cheerfulness and Thomas More was one. Again, in the words of Erasmus, "There is no man so melancholy that he does not gladden." He had a genius for friendship: "he seems born and created for friendship which he cultivates most sincerely and fosters most steadfastly". Should anyone want a finished example of true friendship he could do no better than seek it in More.

His zest for life with its concomitant cheerfulness, that is the dominant impression he makes on me and that is the impression of him I want to leave with you this morning. He found life worth living and death worth dying. As H. A. L. Fisher says, "His end was of a peace with his life, sweetened by innocent mirth and unaffected piety". He could say of his prison, the Tower of London: "Is not this house as nigh heaven as my own". His zest and his cheerfulness were rooted in his faith and trust in God. It has been well said, there is no dull saint, and certainly Thomas More is an illustration of the saying. Few men in our history are so attractive in all their cheerful acceptance of misfortune, the zest of life was his, from youth to the time when he was led from the Tower to suffer the supreme penalty of fidelity to conscience. No misfortune ever robbed him of it. When his house in Chelsea was burnt down he bade his wife be of good cheer and thank God for what still was theirs. And he added with a zest that comes from joy even in the day of misfortune: "I pray you Alice to be merry in God". Surely such a man has learned the secret of zest in companionship of the Lord of life. Here then is the message and the challenge of this service today; to capture that sweet and cheerful spirit that breathed through the life and character of Sir Thomas More; to be merry in God; to learn in Christ that zest that gives life its savour. And whatsoever you do, do it heartily as unto the Lord.

THE RIGHT REVEREND AND RIGHT HONOURABLE ROBERT WRIGHT STOPFORD, K.C.V.O., C.B.E., D.D.

LORD BISHOP OF LONDON

5 JULY 1964

Scholar Hertford College, Oxford. B.A. 1924, M.A. 1927. Honorary Fellow 1956. D.C.L. 1951. D.D. (Lambeth) 1957. Fellow Kings College 1966. C.B.E. 1949. Privy Councillor 1961. Principal Trinity College, Kandy, 1935–40. Principal of Achimota College Gold Coast 1940–45. Honorary Canon of Canterbury 1951–56. Chaplain to H.M. the Queen 1952–55. Chairman Schools Council 1956–58. Consecrated Lord Bishop Suffragan of Fulham 1955. Translated to Peterborough 1956, to London 1961: Resigned 1973. Select Preacher University of Oxford 1963; Cambridge 1963. Dean of Chapels Royal and Prelate of Order of the British Empire 1961. Vicar-General in Jerusalem 1974–76.

On the above date, the More Chapel, furnished with an altar table of about 1620 and re-seated, was dedicated by Robert Stopford, Bishop of London and brought into use again as a Lady Chapel for probably the first time in 408 years.

11

If the foundations are destroyed what can they that are righteous do.

Psalm 11. 3 (New Psalter)

THIS verse seems to give the key to the life of the man of great and unusual gifts who is in our thoughts tonight. This Church we know was very dear to Thomas from the time he moved from his former home in the City in Bucklersbury to Chelsea. This Chapel was the one which he himself restored in 1528. Here in this Church in 1534 he received Holy Communion before he took boat to Lambeth, where the issue was formed on him which led to his arrest and his imprisonment and to his execution. Perhaps the last view he had of the Chelsea he had come to love was of the Church which stood on this site.

For Thomas More religion was part of the very fabric of his life—and therein lies in part at least the explanation of his hold upon the imagination and affection of English people to this day. He is remembered not only for the imagination of his writing, the beauty of his home life and the heroism of his death—but for something more—even though the verdicts of historians on the consistency of his political thinking and action have varied so greatly. Froude saw in him one who persecuted others from mistaken zeal. Acton judged him as the former Apostle of Toleration who allowed his sentiments to be moulded by the official theology of the Court. Mandell Creighton's verdict is much harsher, "It was neither mistaken zeal nor intellectual error that fostered persecution, it was merely expediency and the thirst for power." Yet Erasmus could write of him "In More's death I seem to have died myself, we had but one soul between us." And Mr. G. K. Chesterton 410 years later wrote, "(More) may come to be counted the greatest Englishman, or at least the greatest historical character, in English history."

Perhaps Professor Chambers was right when he said that More's critics have not realised how many of the things in defence of which, at the end of his life, he stepped forward, had already seemed to him so vital when he wrote *Utopia*. It is essential to remember that in *Utopia* More, for all his criticisms of the abuses of the mediaeval experiments in corporate life, wanted not to abolish but to reform them. He was essentially a mediaevalist—not a progressive who changed into a

77

reactionary, but one who believed intensely in the unity of Christendom, and in the peace of Europe and of the Church. As he saw the policy of King Henry VIII striking at the foundations of all that he believed in, and on which everything that was vital for unity was built, his own righteousness forced him to take the stand he did. He could not go with the Reformers because he believed that Reason is servant to Faith not enemy. In *Utopia* he based his whole argument on the belief that Faith in God and in the immortal destiny of the human soul supplies the driving power which is to quench human passion and human greed. In that belief he never wavered in spite of the apparent inconsistencies whch life as the King's servant—and in the end as Chancellor—forced upon him.

The crucial point in his whole life and thought was his denial that the Head of State might dictate the religious belief of his subjects. This comes out early in the *Dialogue of Comfort* which he wrote in prison—it was embodied in his last words on the scaffold on 6th July, 1535—that they should pray for him in this world and he would pray for them elsewhere, protesting that he died "the King's good Servant but God's first."

Thomas More was executed because he challenged the omnicompetence of the state embodied in the person of the King he had tried to serve faithfully and well. All his learning and legal knowledge, all the skill and charity he showed as Sheriff of the City and as Chancellor of the Realm had been for the service of others. His writings give ample proof of this—as do his simplicity of life in the great house he built in the Chelsea meadows, and the personal austerities which he practised. But there was a point beyond which he could not go. "If the foundations are destroyed what can they that are righteous do?" He loved England deeply but he loved Europe too—Europe as Professor Einstein described it "not the Geographical conception but a certain attitude to life and society." In *Utopia* More describes the difference between the men who merely obey the laws of the state and the men who have a belief that there is an ultimate standard of right and wrong beyond what the state may at any moment command. To that same point Cranmer came on the last day of his life when he renounced things written with his hand contrary to the truth which he thought in his heart!

It is always dangerous to draw parallels between one century and another—to seek to find in the attitude of a man in the 16th century the clue to our actions in the 20th century. But this perhaps may be said— Today we accept the idea of a planned society as the only alternative to chaos: though we may differ in our enthusiasm for planning we do not question that in some form it is inevitable. And then we come face to face with the problem—how within this planned society can a place be found for personal integrity and independence of spirit. Perhaps the modern restiveness against authority is due to the subconscious realisation that it is a danger to personality—like some of our fellow Christians in other less free lands than ours.

We may come to the point where we feel that the foundations are destroyed—what then, can we with our minimal righteousness do? That every man must answer in the strength of his own faith. Perhaps in this very Church More wrestled with his conscience. At the time of his trial he said when taunted with cowardice because he would not speak out plain—he replied, "that he had not been a man of such holy living that he might be told to offer himself to death—lest God for my presumption might suffer me to fall. Howbeit if God draw me to it Himself then trust I in His great mercy that He shall not fail to give me grace and strength."

That is the man whose name is linked with the Church. That is the man whom we honour in the rededication of the Chapel which he once restored. That is the man whose example may help us to use more fully in prayer and worship and meditation this Chapel now restored to use: may it become as dear to us as it was to him.

THE REVEREND JACK WALTER MILLER VYSE

VICAR OF THE GUILD CHURCH OF ST. MARY ABCHURCH

4 JULY 1965

Scholar Corpus Christi College, Cambridge,
B.A. 1937, M.A. 1941. Vicar of St. Mary
Abchurch in the City and Diocese of London
from 1961. Vicar of Aylsham, Norwich.

12

THE Roman Catholic writer, Hans Küng, may be known already to some of you for his writings on the Vatican Council, writings which have revealed an unusual understanding of the non-Roman point of view. Now, as a German, as well as a Roman Catholic, he has shown similar understanding of our English way of life, of our history and of our attitudes in one of a series of Meditations published very recently in this country under his editorship. He is concerned in his *Freiheit in der Welt*—Freedom in the World—with the example of Sir Thomas More. His little book has as its frontispiece a reproduction of the Holbein portrait, and he asks: "Is this the face of a 'saint'?". He goes on—"It is indeed a wonderful face: the eyes are serenely thoughtful, critical, you might almost say sceptical, yet not hard, but kindly; the nose and mouth indicate discipline and moderation, unforced assurance and firmness; the whole is of a simple, natural cast, making it a likeable face. A fine, strong face; but a saint's face?".

For Hans Küng, Sir Thomas More is a recognisable Englishman of his time. Attracted by the "positive potentialities of monasticism", he yet marries twice, and has a number of children; he rises to the top of his profession as a lawyer, and goes not unrewarded in material things and in fame. And yet this apparent negation of the three marks of "perfection"—chastity, poverty and obedience—may justifiably be seen as the fulfilment of them all, in a chaste and happy family life, in a generous stewardship of his wordly goods, and the fundamental discipline of living of which his famous—or notorious—hair shirt is but a symbol. Indeed, he may be said to have done what his Lord required of him, to have dealt justly, to have shown mercy, and to have walked humbly with his God. But is this the face of a saint? Is this the manner of a saint?

I am not concerned now with whether we ought to speak of him as a saint or as a knight, as Saint Thomas, or Sir Thomas. But by any standard known to a Christian, this man is a saint, if by that we mean a dedicated person, a person doing his duty conscientiously to God and to man; whether obviously to God in his regular service at the altar in this very church, or obviously to man in the City of London, and in the High Courts of this realm—if he, or we, can allow such a dichotomy of service, such an arbitrary separation of the sacred and the secular. We may remember, and may well be puzzled by, the final act of conscience which brought him, almost obstinately we may think, to his death. We may, because we are shocked by the whole business, fall back on feeling that it could never happen now—some way would have been found, he might have resigned his offices and kept at least his life if not his freedom. But it is not as easy as that. We cannot in our own day admire Bonhoeffer and Stauffenberg and the rest for their opposition to Hitler, and, at the same time, suggest that Sir Thomas was really pressing things a little too far. The trouble is that while we may admire the modern martyrs, we shudder at the thought of being asked ever to follow their example. We are prepared to pay lip service to the idea of seeking first the Kingdom of God—but by no means so ready to admit that some of the things consequently to be added unto us may be violently uncomfortable. There may come a time when we may hate the next step, but it must be taken. Thomas More may well have hoped to find some modus vivendi with his king, but he knew from the moment he took his stand just how much was involved and just how much he was risking.

The face of a saint? A lot of the tests of our saintliness happen on what we may call the frontiers of our own experience, where to give a little may be charity, to give a little more may be expedient and justifiable—part, as we say, of the long term policy, part of the justifying means: but where to give beyond a certain limit is not only foolish but wrong, not only inadvisable but sinful, where integrity and truth are in question, where, commit ourselves though we may to the probability of blood and sweat and toil and tears, the answer must nevertheless be "so far and no further".

Lest you misunderstand this, as some romantic ideal, some frontier we may never reach, can we remember that a frontier is not just a matter of well known checkpoints where the headline events take place? Our lives are full of, so to say, the minor border incidents, each one absolute and perilous in its own way. We stand to be challenged at any point; and at any point we may pretend to be less than we are, and, drawing the cloak of disguise over our conscience, pass safely through. This can be the greyness of the safe and secure compromise of which, as Anglicans, we are so often accused. And who shall dare not to say that sometimes we deserve it?

Sir Thomas More fell under the accusation of treason because he would not accept his king in place of the Pope as the head of the Church on earth. We live in days when there seems to be an ever closer rapprochement between Papists and Anglicans, and we rightly emphasise all that we have in common. But we must not lose sight of the fact that here to-day we are commemorating a man who died, officially as a traitor, for resisting precisely that form of establishment which we as Anglicans

82

regard as part of God's will for the Church in this country. The conference table may now have taken the place of the execution block, but we must not delude ourselves that there are no difficulties, no points of division left. The most catholicly minded of us must not be ashamed of our protestantism. We must not be afraid still to agree with the Article and, believing that in some respects the Church of Rome—and other churches—has erred; continue to be Protestant against such error. We may regret that things came to such a pass for Sir Thomas More; but we must acknowledge that, in respect at least, we could not have stood alongside him.

What is important for us is that we should see his stand, however much we may disagree with his reasons for it, as his final refusal to compromise with what he—in this case perhaps wrongly, perhaps rightly—felt to be wrong. His death was in no sense the result of a sudden obstinacy, but the natural and inevitable application of a consistent attitude, adopted and stuck to and lived by, long before in all sorts of situations. We may assume that often before in his career, in his relationships with his family and his friends, he had similarly risked misunderstanding and unpopularity, had chosen the harder rather than the easier way, perhaps against his personal liking; hating what he felt forced to do, sighing for the persons or the circumstances that made his action necessary. We know of the stand he took when he was only twenty-five in the House of Commons, when he thought the demands of his king for money unjust; of how "the beardless boy . . . made such arguments and reasons there against" that they "were thereby clean overthrown". How many other such incidents were there in which he chose "rather to suffer affliction with the people of God", when he valued the praise of God more than the praise of men?

A deatnbed martyrdom could mean as little as a deathbed repentance. What matters is the assurance of a good conscience throughout the whole of a man's life. Edith Cavell, of whom we have been reminded in this past week, can no more be judged only by her behaviour before the firing squad fifty years ago than can Sir Thomas More only by his behaviour before his executioner. "Now is the judgement of this world" means for each one of us a judgement in accordance with every one of our acts, of our decisions, our thoughts, our words, our deeds, our moral judgements—each of them made as though it were our last.

"They that stand high have many winds to shake them", and we have continued to see the fall of public figures, political falls and moral falls. They fall now—as they have often now to make their fateful decisions—in the full glare of modern publicity. And yet we are moved, as no doubt England was moved by what happened at the Tower on the 6th of July 430 years ago.

But the real point is that day by day, minute by minute, men and women are making decisions which will never hit a single headline; and each of them is a judgement here and now on themselves as individuals—and so cumulatively on the whole society of which we are part. In this sense, as in so many others, when one member suffers the whole body suffers with it.

How often in this last week have you kept quiet when you should have spoken out for what is true or right or just? How often by our sins has justice or truth gone simply by default? How many of us have one standard for our family, one standard for our friends, and another for our job? How many of us show any real sense of responsibility? How many of us really earn what we are paid? How many of us are completely honest? How many of us could claim to be really moral? Which is the voice that we obey; our conscience, or convenience? our own, or God's?

To Wolsey, broken—certainly for very different reasons—on the same royal rock as Sir Thomas More, Shakespeare gives the remorseful words:
" . . . Be just, and fear not;
Let all the ends thou aim'st at be thy country's,
Thy God's, and truth's: then if thou fall'st . . .
Thou fall'st a blessed martyr."

Such cynicism—for so we may feel it—could well have been addressed to Thomas Cromwell. For Thomas More Shakespeare could not put into Wolsey's mouth other than the wish:
" May he continue
Long in his highness' favour, and do justice
For truth's sake and for his conscience. . . ."

That word "Conscience" haunts us as we keep this face—this saint's face?—of Thomas More before our minds. As we commemorate him, as we pray that he may now rest in peace, we may remember, for our own assurance, what he himself wrote of his Utopians:
"They thinke that this remembrance of the vertue and goodness of the dead doeth vehemently provoke and enforce the living to virtue. And that nothing be more pleasaunt and acceptable to the deade. Whom they suppose to be present among them, when they talke of them, though to the dull and feble eiesight of mortall men they be invisible."

And so—"Requiescat in pace"—May he rest in peace.

CANON ALFONSO DE ZULUETA
RECTOR OF THE CHURCH OF OUR MOST HOLY REDEEMER AND SAINT THOMAS MORE

3 JULY 1966

New College, Oxford. B.A. 1926, M.A.
1931. Roman Catholic Chaplain at University of Oxford 1939–41. Rector of our Most
Holy Redeemer and Saint Thomas More,
Chelsea, from 1945. Honorary Canon of
Westminster Cathedral 1966. Chapter
Canon from 1976.

———

The award-winning feature film *A Man for
All Seasons* was first shown in 1966. Directed
by Fred Zinnemann to Robert Bolt's script,
Paul Scofield starred as Thomas More,
Wendy Hiller as Alice, Leo McKern as
Cromwell, Robert Shaw as Henry VIII,
Orson Welles as Cardinal Wolsey and Susannah York as Margaret. Six Oscars were won.

13

"Well loved of God,
Well loved of Men,
A blessing rests upon his memory."

These words are taken from the Book of Ecclesiasticus, the 45th Chapter, the first verse.

MR. Mayor, dearly beloved brethren in Jesus Christ. You can imagine what a very great joy it is to accept the very kind and generous invitation from your Vicar that I should address you to-day.

First of all I come to you as your fellow Christian. I don't come from very far in point of distance as you know; we're all good friends and neighbours already, but you understand how much greater is the distance we have all travelled in the last few years since the Oecumenical Movement, since Pope John, since this wind of the Holy Spirit has been blowing through the whole of Christendom, to show us the will of our Lord and Saviour, "that they may all be one, even as Thou Father art in Me and I in Thee, that all men may believe that Thou hast sent me." And we have come, all of us, to realise something of the terrible scandal of our disunity. This it is which has made us all realise the importance of what we have in common, the tremendous grace of our Christian Baptism, and at the same time, if our ecumenism and our search for unity is going to be true and sincere, then we must seek the truth in the Church as Brothers. Because this new relationship is not mere politeness—which can be a rather cold thing—but is a warm Christian love and charity, and therefore as the members of a family we must explain in all love and amity what are the differences that still remain between us.

In this year as you know there has been this quite unparalleled event since the Reformation of the meeting in Rome between Pope Paul VI and Michael, Archbishop of Canterbury. And they have made there this solemn declaration which I would just like to quote to you at the beginning of our thoughts on Thomas More.

"In willing obedience of the command of Christ who bade his disciples love one another, they declare that with His help they wish to

87

leave in the hands of the God of mercy all that has in the past been opposed to this precept of Charity, and that they make their own the mind of the Apostle which he expressed in these terms—'forgetting those things which are behind and reaching forward unto those things which are before, I press toward the mark of the high calling of God in Jesus Christ.'"

They affirm their desire that all those Christians who belong to these two communions may be animated by the same sentiments of respect, esteem and mutual love, and in order to help these develop to the full they intend to inaugurate between the Roman Catholic Church and the Anglican Communion a serious dialogue which, founded on the Gospels and on the ancient common traditions, may lead to that Unity and Truth for which Christ prayed.

The Pope and the Archbishop went on to say that they were well aware of the serious difficulties in doctrine and in practice which still remain. But placing all their confidence in the Holy Spirit and guided, as they firmly believe, by Him, they continue this search for truth. And I must say that, speaking locally, I have found the fraternals, the various dialogues and discussions which we have between Ministers and lay people of all denominations, most helpful. One learns a great deal from them I am sure on both sides. And we come to see how very often certain things have only been misunderstandings, of these questions of practice, there are undoubtedly other things that still remain questions of principle. But all these things, by the Grace of the Holy Spirit, we pray may one day before very long be brought to a happy understanding.

Then I come to you also of course as a fellow citizen of Chelsea. Mr. Mayor will pardon the inaccuracy of the expression. "A citizen of no mean city." We love so much our little village as it once was, the character still retained by the river, that very river down which Thomas More went on his last journey, a journey to the Tower. This village of palaces as it was called, which is known all over the world not only for its football club, but is known for its art, its individuality, its freedom from, shall we say, restricting conventions, because there are conventions which are, after all, helpful. But nevertheless its freedom, its sense of being something different from other people—was that perhaps in some sense a legacy of Thomas More? It would be nice to think so. Because in the third place I come particularly this evening as a fellow lover and admirer of Thomas More.

We can all unite in our admiration not only of him as a charming man, a family man, a great humanist, one of the most charming and delightful characters that has ever existed. Even Erasmus, who was certainly hard to please, a most critical person, said that Nature had never framed anything more delightful, more pleasant, more gentle than Thomas More.

88

But, of course, we also can admire More's stand for conscience, for the freedom of the individual and the Christian, from any external secular tyranny. Then his great defence of the indissolubility of marriage, and the sacred character of Christian marriage, because this of course was the hub of the question between him and Henry. There is no anger like that of a woman scorned they say, and Anne Boleyn urged Henry, where he might have, for old friendship's sake, not demanded that oath which was against More's conscience. As he said to the Lords when they pronounced judgement—"I know that even more than the supremacy it is for the marriage that you seek my blood."

And then of course he was one who dies for the ideal of the unity of Christendom and the unity of the Church. I am here of course, speaking frankly as a Roman Catholic Priest. I naturally share the view that More shared, that there is a divinely appointed centre of unity in the Church, and the remarkable thing is that More could see that in Popes, not like Pope John and Pope Paul—the sort of Popes we have had for a very long time now—but in people like Alexander VI, and Leo X, and Clement VII, who were hardly advertisements for their sacred office. He saw beneath those outward appearances to what we believe to be the Rock of Peter.

In this matter obviously we are not agreed, but nevertheless there is, I know, a new respect, a new understanding for what that centre of unity wishes to be, as the Pope has so very clearly repeated, both Pope John and Pope Paul, "not in any spirit of ambition or domination but as the Servant of the servants of God we wish to be of service to all, and to serve humbly and to take all Christians as we find them, to help them, to be their servant".

Now what sort of man was Thomas More? What sort of a man was this man who dared to stand up to a King like Henry? When men like the Duke of Norfolk, like the Bishop of London, were asked for advice by the Carthusian monks, there was only one answer—Ira Principis Morta Est— The anger of the Prince means death. That was the only answer that most of them had. And we have to place ourselves in their position. We mustn't be too hard on them, we know that, not only because the prestige of the Papacy had sunk so low they were confused in their minds and so on, even though Convocation for the first time only accepted the King's Supremacy by inserting the clause—"so far as the law of Christ allows." We know Henry wasn't having any of that, and out it came, and that was why Bishop Fisher, alone amongst the Bishops, and Thomas More alone amongst laymen, refused to take it in that form. But More was a person who was not out for martyrdom, and I think this is very helpful to average Christians like ourselves, because you know the sort of people who go around saying—"I'd love to be a martyr," then, when the time comes perhaps they feel rather differently. And Thomas More was a man of such

89

true ecumenity that he always felt, (and he said it in those letters that he has written to his daughter from the Tower) that he was very much afraid of himself, he was very much afraid of his human weakness, of his great fear of pain, of the terrible death of a traitor. He was also a man of great loyalty to his King, and therefore even the slightest implication of a lack of loyalty was extremely painful to him. Moreover he had this strong affection and complete family life, centred here in Chelsea a few yards from here, bounded pretty well by Danvers Street at one end, by Milman Street on the other, in the centre of Beaufort Street where we have that Convent of Nuns who pray day and night for the world and for Chelsea. There was the house of Thomas More, the great house he built himself in 1525, with his wonderful collection of family, relatives, friends, people he took into his house for the sake of Charity; animals, a whole menagerie, monkeys, all sorts of curious things. This happy world was certainly something he didn't want to leave unless he had to. And therefore, as a very astute and able lawyer, he took his stand on the fact that treason could not be found in silence, that nobody had a right to compel him to take an oath which was against his conscience, but that he would not give the reason. And it was only after he was found guilty that he spoke out, made his profession of belief, and gave the reasons which made him refuse to take the oath. Because there was one point, one radical point, (whatever one thinks of his particular convictions) which every Christian, and I would even say every good man whatever his religion, must agree with: never willingly, as he put it, "to cast myself damnably in the displeasure of God."

The foundation of his whole life was the idea that God is the supreme end of man. "This is God and His whole law, obey God and keep His commandments for this is the whole duty of man." These words of Scripture were keenly engraved upon his mind and heart, and were his whole point through this great agony of mind that he must have. We can imagine it, in this house in Chelsea surrounded by people who entirely depended on him, whom he loved dearly, whom he couldn't for a long time even take into his confidence. The one thing he never swerved from, as he told his daughter, was that he must always obey his conscience, because in obeying the voice of his conscience he was obeying the voice of God, and that the supreme end of man is to obey God, and those terrible words of the Gospel were in his ears—"If any love his father and mother more than me he is not worthy of me—he that will save his life shall lose it, and he that will lose his life for my sake shall find it unto life eternal." This was the quite simple principle that he was guided by. And as he meditated, as he studied, as he thought the whole thing over from every different angle during those increasingly difficult years, he came to this conclusion— I cannot do this, whatever it costs me I cannot do it—and in that of course resides the Saint. A Saint is not a person devised primarily for stained glass windows, somebody rather unreal and of another world than ourselves, a Saint is a whole man. It's rather interesting because in English the word "holy" comes from the same root as "whole" "complete" "entire". And therefore our common human nature cannot, without greatness, achieve its full perfection. That was the failure of the Greeks and of all those who have built fine and noble civilisations, but without divine revelation. It was only the Divine Revelation coming to us through the Old Testament, and supremely through Jesus Christ, that could enable us to achieve this intimate communion with God, this partaking of the Divine Nature to which we are admitted at Baptism, through the merits of Jesus Christ, and with which we have to correspond in the light of grace. And therefore a Saint will be a man who has tried, with God's help, however imperfectly, consistently up to the moment of his death, the supreme moment which we all have to face, and which is the moment, we hope, of our beginning. "In my end," as Mary Queen of Scots said, "is my beginning". That supreme moment is built up to and prepared for by a life of completeness, by a life of grace.

And so when to look at the life of Thomas More we discover that under all that gaiety, under that pleasantness of manner, under that cheerfulness, there was a profound life of prayer, that learned from the Carthusian monks in the London Charterhouse when he was a young man and lodged with them, and seriously thought of entering their life, and then reflecting and thinking over he realised that in the Church there are these two ways, the life of virginity, the life dedicated in a very special way by the renunciation of the ordinary legitimate pleasures of life, to Almighty God, and then on the other hand the other way, the normal way for most people, the way of the married life, and in either of those you can achieve this holiness to which God calls you. The important thing is not to make the mistake and to go into the wrong one. And therefore he freely chose the married life, having freely chosen the service of the State, not out of personal ambition, but simply because he believed that, in that way he could serve God. He kept up all his life the life of prayer (he even built himself a little cottage, a little building in the garden here where he could get right away from everyone and pray). He supported continuously his Parish Church. You remember when the Duke of Norfolk came and found him in a surplice singing in the choir and said "God's Body, God's Body, my Lord Chancellor—a Parish Clerk, a Parish Clerk!!" And he said, "It seems to me my Lord the King's Majesty is honoured by my service of his Master and mine." And you see that was always the thing, that the King was not the Supreme Being, always God first, the King's good servant, but God's first.

In 1935 Pope Pius XI decided to repay a debt that had long been owing from the Roman Catholic Church to Thomas More, and a debt in which all Christians have willingly concurred in seeing a very fitting action. The canonisation of a Saint only means that as far as the Church can tell he is one of those people who have exercised heroic virtue up to the time of their death, and who are Saints of God in Heaven. There are, thank God, millions of people in the Communion of Saints whose names we don't even know, please God many of our nearest and dearest. The Church selects some of these flowers from God's garden, puts some of these lamps upon a pedestal that they may shine to the whole house. And this was done not only as a gesture towards Thomas More, as a gesture of goodwill towards the English people, but there is a very interesting sideline to it. In 1935 the Nazi Movement in Germany was at its height, the Pope was about to issue his great encyclical against the errors of the Nazi creed, (it came out in 1937), and this action was understood very well in Germany where amongst Christians it gave great comfort, and to the Government gave great displeasure. Its significance was well understood. At that time Hitler visited Rome and the Pope openly absented himself saying that he would not remain in a city where the crooked cross, opposed to the Cross of Christ, was flaunted. That is an interesting sideline to the background of the canonisation coming at exactly that time.

On Saturday we shall be having our usual procession with the relic of Thomas More from our Church, the Holy Redeemer and St. Thomas, to the Convent in Beaufort Street which is more or less on the site of his house. And in this procession, we realise of course all of us, that the relic of a Saint is nothing in itself, simply the implication of the Christian belief that that body has been the Temple of the Holy Ghost, that it will rise again in a new body, that man is a double being—body as well as soul. The whole religion of the Incarnation and the sacramental outlook presupposes that we honour the body in that sense. But really our honour is that honour in which we all join to-day, to the wonderful and yet at the same time very ordinary, holiness of Thomas More, the man who was able to take the decision he did because all his life he had been singularly dedicated to God, because his whole life he had loved Him above all things. And that though he dreaded that terrible choice that all Christians have got to be ready to expect between those one loves most, and God to Whom we owe that love, from Whom all good things come. He was afraid that this choice would come. He wasn't going to rush into it, he wasn't a Thomas of Canterbury who we might say in a sense rushed into it, was a fighter by nature. More was not like that. Only when the last ditch came—"I can't disobey my God. I remain the King's good servant always, but God's first."

92

CANON ALAN LESLIE LAWLER

CANON OF CANTERBURY CATHEDRAL

9 JULY 1967

A.K.C. 1934. University of London, B.D.
1934. Public Preacher Diocese of Chelms-
ford 1939–40. Proctor in Convocation
Canterbury 1950–55. Vicar of St. Dunstan
City and Diocese of Canterbury from 1954.
Canon of Canterbury Cathedral.

14

THE fifty second verse of the thirteenth chapter of St. Matthew's Gospel from the New English Bible: "When a teacher of the law has become a learner in the Kingdom of Heaven, he is like a householder who can produce from his store both the new and the old."

First, may I say how grateful I am for the honour of being allowed to preach on this occasion, when we remember with thanksgiving one who had an intimate connection with your parish and with mine, and from my parish, St. Dunstan of the Holy Cross, Canterbury, I bring you greetings. And I will also congratulate you on the mounting success of your endeavour to provide for posterity a fitting memorial of a great English Christian and statesman.

To return to my text "When a teacher of the law has become a learner in the Kingdom of Heaven, he is like a householder who can produce from his store both the new and the old." Sir Thomas More is well described as a teacher of the law and a learner in the Kingdom of Heaven and a householder who can produce from his store both the new and the old.

As to the old, there is in him something that calls to mind thoughts of the prophets of old. There is, for instance, something reminiscent of John the Baptist; metaphorically speaking, I underline the word "reminiscent" for it would be untrue to say that he was like John the Baptist. In that greatest of all the prophets there is, according to the record in the Gospels no suggestion at all of an inkling of a sense of humour. His fascination for the crowds was rather that of the snake for the rabbit. Thomas More's sense of humour was such that his critics could accuse him of a lack of proper seriousness. "These jests", said Lord Herbert of Cherbury, and of course he was referring to the rather light-hearted way in which Thomas More spoke of the future of himself and his family when he resigned the Chancellorship, "these jests were thought to have in them more levity than to be taken everywhere for current. He might have acquit his dignity without using such sarcasms and betaken himself to a more retired and quiet life without making them (his family) or himself contemptible." Nor did his sense of humour desert him on the scaffold: "I pray you, I pray you, Mr. Lieutenant, see me safe up, and for my coming down, let me shift for myself." Yet the hair-shirt which he is reputed always to have worn shows that like John the Baptist, Thomas More was something of an ascetic, though his ascetism was not without purpose nor was it devoid of joy. To his Utopians, and who can doubt that the thought represents his own mind, it was not only madness but ingratitude to God to waste the body by fasting or to forego the pleasures of life unless by doing so a man can serve others and promote their happiness.

But more important than the ascetism which he shared with John the Baptist was the fact that like him—and here I use phrases which you will recognise from the Collect of St. John Baptist's Day—Thomas More constantly spoke the truth, boldly rebuked vice and patiently suffered for the truth's sake. And this is primarily what we remember Sir Thomas More for. It was his concern for truth and his opposition to what he believed to be wrong which led him to suffer patiently, on more than one occasion in his life, and finally on Tower Hill on July 6th 1535.

If, on the one hand, Thomas More had affinities with the past, on the other, it would also be true to say that in many ways he would be at home in the world of today. It is clear from his writings, as well as from his life, that he would be entirely in sympathy with those who in these days urge us to break down the false barriers between the sacred and the secular, the spiritual and the material. The Utopia can hardly be regarded as his picture of the ideal world, bearing in mind for instance what his own profession was; the suggestion "utterly to exclude and banish all Attorneys, Proctors and Sergeants at the Law, which craftily handle matters and subtly dispute of the laws", must have been made with his tongue in cheek. The Utopia is not so much a blueprint for the future as a satirical comment on the times in which he lived. Nevertheless, it can be said to show that for Thomas More, there is no part of life outside a Christian's concern. He deals among other things with politics, economics, international relationships, working conditions and even sanitation. He sees the Christian as necessarily involved in the life of the world, and it is significant that he does not emphasise this truth, he does not shout it from the housetops, he simply takes it for granted. Yet he did not, as some of our modern prophets are inclined to do, give the impression that the whole Gospel is summed up in the pre-Christian, Old Testament injunction "Thou shalt love thy neighbour as thyself". He knew that love of neighbour depends upon love of God and that our love for God and neighbour depends on his love for us.

There are no doubt many today who seeing the practical nature of his faith, would welcome Thomas More as an ally. They might not quite so easily appreciate the depth of his devotional life. We learn from William Roper, his son-in-law, of my parish, that daily family prayer was his custom, and that after this he would say the seven Psalms, the Litany and the Suffrages, and at night he would take his family to chapel for Psalms and Collects. This on an ordinary weekday. On Fridays, the whole day was passed in chapel, and I quote again, spending his time in devout prayers and spiritual exercises.

Few have given more of themselves in service to mankind than Sir Thomas More. More people might give more, if they had a little more of his spirit of devotion.

Another way in which Sir Thomas More was far in advance of his time was in his interest in science, and in his readiness to accept new discoveries without seeing in them an inevitable threat to the faith of the Church. Searching out the secrets of nature the Utopians regarded as peculiarly acceptable to God. To realise how far he was ahead of his time, one only has to think for instance of the controversies of the nineteenth century, particularly those which had to do with evolution, which was supposed by many completely to undermine the whole basis of the Christian doctrine of creation. And it is perhaps little wonder that a nineteenth century Bishop—Creighton—to whom More was certainly not a hero, described him as "a typical instance of that pseudo-liberalism so common at all times which obscures and confuses every question it touches", a description which has been repeated almost word for word for certain people living today.

Earlier, a contemporary, William Tyndall, describes More as one ". . . who knew the truth and forsook it again". For Sir Thomas More there were no final and authoritative answers; his mind was open to truth whatever its source, for he believed all truth ultimately to be of God. He was not, however, the kind of man of whom perhaps there are some today who would welcome only the new and question only the old. Nor did he suppose that science had all the answers to life's questions, but he did welcome the contribution that science can make towards the totality of our knowledge of God and his world. He was, if you like, a radical who dug down to the roots, but he did not dig the roots up and throw them away, for he was also conservative of all that was true and good from the past. In his person he summed up all that is best in our Anglican tradition: he valued the truth handed down from the past. He also welcomed new truths and new ideas.

And so at this time we commemorate a great Christian and a great statesman, one who made a tremendous contribution to the life both of church and of nation. And we do it in a time when we are often bewildered by the growth of new knowledge, and by the rapidity of scientific discovery, so that at times the very foundation of our faith appears to be shaken. But may there be in us something of the temper that there was in

97

Sir Thomas More, to enable us to hold fast to the old truths and to welcome the new. May we, like him, though we may not be teachers of the law, yet be learners in the Kingdom of Heaven and produce from our store both the new and the old.

PROFESSOR HOWARD EUGENE ROOT

PROFESSOR OF THEOLOGY IN THE UNIVERSITY OF SOUTHAMPTON

7 JULY 1968

St. Catherine's Society, Oxford, B.A. 1951. Magdalen College Oxford 1952. Magdalene College, Cambridge, M.A. 1953. Fellow Emmanuel College, Cambridge Chaplain 1954–56, Dean 1956–66. Select Preacher University of Cambridge 1957. Hulsean Preacher University of Cambridge 1961. Proctor in Convocation University of Cambridge 1965–66. Professor of Theology University of Southampton and Public Preacher Diocese of Winchester from 1966. Honorary Canon of Winchester Cathedral 1966–67, Canon Theologian from 1967. Official Anglican Observer at Second Vatican Council. Member of the Academic Council, Ecumenical Institute for Advanced Studies, Jerusalem from 1966. Member of the Anglican-Roman Catholic International Commission from 1969.

A bronze plaque, set in the floor of Westminster Hall to commemorate Thomas More's trial there, was unveiled jointly by the Lord Chancellor, Lord Gardiner, and the Speaker of the House of Commons, Dr. Horace King, on 13 March 1968.

15

IT is a privilege for me to be in this historic church at your commemoration of that sainted figure, Thomas More. Simply to remember him is enough to humble any man. But there is another feature in our commemoration today which I think provides something of a key to its contemporary meaning. We have, as the Vicar has said, with us, His Excellency Archbishop Cardinale, the personal representative of Pope Paul in this land. And what, one wonders, would Thomas More make of that. Perhaps at no time from More's troubled sixteenth century until our day, could such a thing have been possible. It is not enough, I think, to pat ourselves on the back and rather self righteously proclaim what splendid open minded chaps we are in comparison with our religious ancestors of four hundred years ago. One cannot but believe that Thomas More, with all the Saints, rejoices at every step we take towards the restoration of christian unity, but we do no honour to More by implying that the kind of issues for which he and his contemporaries were willing to die were not really all that important and that we are much more sophisticated about such things in these days. For sophisticated you might read indifferent. The life and faith and martyrdom of Thomas More stand before us as a kind of challenge and warning and judgement. We can't get inside his skin and see his problems precisely as he saw them, simply because we are men of our own time, the twentieth century, not of his; nor I suppose do we feel with such sharpness some of the theological argument of the reformation and counter-reformation period. Sufficient unto each age are no doubt its problems. But there are qualities which transcend the barriers of time and cultural differences.

We revere More for his learning, the learning of a humanist in the true and proper christian sense, for his courage and loyalty, for his extraordinary gentleness and lightness, almost, of heart and wit, but above all for that depth of faith and love for God, which we can only call his sanctity. Perhaps one sees both the sanctity and irrepressible spirit in those words he's recorded as having spoken to the judges who had just condemned him to death: "We may yet," he said, "we may yet hereafter in heaven merrily meet together to everlasting salvation." He found conscience a hard master but his charity forbad him to dishonour the consciences of others. And these are some of the themes from the life of More which speak to our condition and which we ignore only at our peril.

101

Let me take this a bit further by raising a question; How, some might ask, how can Anglicans genuinely and without dissimulation revere Thomas More as man and saint? Of course, anyone can appreciate noble human qualities in a man of some other christian obedience or of some other religion or no religion at all. But beyond that does not the special testimony of More in his own time carry a kind of threat to the Anglican tradition? Well, there's an easy facile answer which some may think good enough. You could say that what we are admiring is just a noble spirit, who as it happens took certain religious matters rather too seriously. You know, just a little bit unbalanced. It would have been much happier if he had not made such a fuss about the royal supremacy, just accepted it. Then his life would have been spared, and think how much good he could have done, and what great influence still he might have exerted. But this is, is it not, only a variant of the common appeal to political expediency. What's the point in resigning from the Government, just because you disagree with this or that policy. Keep your job and then see how much more good you can do from inside instead of landing yourself outside. It's the kind of argument we hear time and time again in connection with politics, or with business, or even with the church and religion."

"Don't take it all seriously. Life's too short. Accommodate yourself. A bit of realism now, a bit of compromise now, and you will be able to do all sorts of good things later." The great philosopher, Immanuel Kant, was fond of saying that mankind could not too often be reminded that there once lived a man called Socrates. And what he meant was that when everybody is saying 'after all I've got to live', remember that Socrates said, 'no, I haven't got to live; not if the price is too high.' Thomas More's answer is the same, and we deceive ourselves if we think that he was just a very good man who, unfortunately, was a bit fanatical. We must try no such evasion. But I think we must allow ourselves to be confronted and our faith judged by the witness of Thomas More. Our faith, if its foundations are secure, is not threatened by that witness. But, it may, God willing, be cleansed and renewed and made more worthy. And the same, I think, surely, would be true, for example for the faithful and loyal Roman Catholic in, say, the commemoration of the Maryon martyrs. It's one thing to be, or to feel threatened. It's quite another to be humbled and brought to self examination. And so throughout the history of the Church, so often beset with human dissension, the figures who have sometimes been the focus for controversy can, in fact, become a focus for common penitence and for common hope of renewal and unity. But there are two points that I think need special emphasis. We thank God for the work of the Holy Spirit in moving us, unprepared and unworthy as we are, along the road to the restoration of christian unity. And, in particular, I think, for what has already been achieved between the See of Rome and the See of Canterbury. The momentous visit of Archbishop to Pope in March of 1966, set the seal on the beginning of a new relationship. If we are to realise our hopes, mutual charity and trust must come first, and amongst other things this means obviously repudiating all polemics, and not, either through suspicion or fear, re-opening old wounds of division. But this does not mean that on either side we are called upon to repudiate our past. It's not for us to say that in the sixteenth century or in any other, that our spiritual ancestors, whether Anglican or Catholic, were simply pigheaded. For one thing it is presumptuous of the sons to confess the sins of their fathers. But more than this, we can't see their problems as they saw them, and we can't say that in the same circumstances we might not have done the same in perfect good faith and with utter integrity. The injustices and cruelties so obvious to us were there no doubt on all sides, but, like More we leave their resolution to God alone.

The second point is very well illustrated by our presence here today. Here we are, an Anglican congregation, in an Anglican church, a church which was also Thomas More's church. It is a place of worship despite the ravages of war. A place of worship which was here before our divisions, and, please God, will be here still when they are finally healed. And further this Anglican commemoration of Thomas More takes place in the presence, and assisted by the prayers, of a Roman Catholic Archbishop. Now, to the outsider it might look a situation full of anomalies and contradictions, but I hope that with the eyes of faith we see it instead as filled with glorious promise. But again I think we must beware self congratulation. In all ecumenical activity there does lurk a potential danger. Namely the danger that ecumenism simply freezes our differences instead of healing them. We find it these days so agreeable, to some unexpectedly agreeable, to be friendly and charitable one to another, but we may be tempted just to settle down cosily in our divisions. After all, if we can get on in so many ways so happily, why press ahead to full unity? Why not settle for something so much easier, so much quicker? and this I think is an insidious attitude, all the more so because people can fall into it hardly aware of what they are doing. And once again, the figure of Thomas More confronts us with a challenge. We may be loyal sons of the churches wherein we were born, and to whom we owe our knowledge of Christ and the perpetual gift of his word and sacraments, but as More insisted, God's will comes first. And it is his unmistakable will that we should be one, in full and perfect communion. We all know that there are enormous difficulties, but our hope is not in ourselves but in God. And we take courage from the sure faith that truth is one and that our common quest for unity in truth cannot finally be frustrated so long as we are faithful, and receptive, and willing to be led into all truth by the Spirit. We take strength in the knowledge that we are compassed about by a great host of witnesses and saints, and can we doubt as believers in the

103

communion of saints, that even as his faith sets our standard, Sir Thomas More rejoices at what we do here. Our commemoration of him is no backward looking gesture. Instead, I think, it reminds us of those words from Saint Paul, which were used by the Archbishop and the Pope in their common declaration. The words from the Third Chapter of Philippians: "forgetting those things which are behind and reaching forth unto those things which are before, I press toward the mark for the prize of the high calling of God in Jesus Christ."

THE LORD ARCHBISHOP OF CANTERBURY THE MOST REVEREND AND RIGHT HONOURABLE ARTHUR MICHAEL RAMSEY, D.D.

PRIMATE OF ALL ENGLAND AND METROPOLITAN

28 JULY 1969

Scholar Magdalene College Cambridge, B.A. 1927, M.A. 1930, B.D. 1950, Hon. D.D. 1957. University of Oxford Honorary D.C.L. 1960. Sub-Warden of Lincoln Theological College 1930–36. Canon of Durham Cathedral and Professor of Divinity University of Durham 1940–50. Regius Professor of Divinity University of Cambridge and Fellow of Magdalene College, Cambridge 1950–52. Select Preacher University of Cambridge 1934, 40, 48, 59, 64, Oxford 1945–47. Consecrated Lord Bishop of Durham 1952: Translated to York 1956, to Canterbury 1961. Resigned 1974. Created Lord Ramsey of Canterbury 1974.

———

The statue of Thomas More, outside the More Chapel of Chelsea Old Church, was unveiled on 21 July 1969 by the Speaker of the House of Commons, Dr. Horace King, in the presence of the Archbishop of Canterbury, Dr. Michael Ramsey, the Cardinal Archbishop of Westminster, Cardinal John Heenan, and the Moderator of the Free Church Federal Council.

16

The First Epistle of St. Paul to the Corinthians, Chapter 1, Verse 3: "Called to be saints."

A WEEK ago on the 21st July, Mr. Speaker unveiled the statue of Thomas More, scholar, statesman, saint, on the Embankment outside the Old Church of Chelsea. Today, you the people of Chelsea make your own commemoration of one for whom Chelsea is always proud. Many great men through the years have had their homes in Chelsea, but perhaps none greater than Thomas More; and it is lovely to think how the chapel which he restored in his own time survived through all the damage and destruction of the terrible years of the last War. We picture Thomas More in the various stages of his stormy career. First we see him at Lambeth Palace as a page to the Archbishop of Canterbury; then we see him as an eager student absorbing as much as he could of the new learning. We see him all the while as a very devout man who at one time thought of being a monk but did not feel that the vocation to celibacy was his. We see him as a family man here in his home in Chelsea, happy with family and friends around him. We see him in public life, Member of Parliament, Speaker of the House of Commons, Lord Chancellor; we see him as the loyal Catholic churchman answering the doctrines of Martin Luther in vigorous writings. We see him as a champion of new learning, welcoming Erasmus and other scholars to his home in Chelsea. We see him as an idealist, dreaming of the future happiness of mankind and depicting in his work, Utopia—an ideal state where men were wise and where men were good and shared the wealth in common for the good of all. And we see him above all, as a man dedicated to righteousness. He withstood the intention of King Henry VIII's divorce; he withstood the new form of the Royal Supremacy feeling that it encroached upon the sovereign rights of the Church of God and in that belief in the end he gave his life.

Let me recall as I did a week ago, the closing scene early in the morning of July 6 1535, Thomas More's singular friend, Thomas Pope, came early to the Tower to tell him that he was to die before nine o'clock and "the King's pleasure is further," said Pope, "that at your execution you should not use many words." And there followed the walk to the scaffold, and very soon the news of Thomas More's last very few words was travelling far and wide. And this is how the most authentic narrator describes it.

"He spoke little before his execution, only he asked the bystanders to pray for him in this world and he would pray for them elsewhere. He then begged them to pray earnestly for the King that it might please God to give him good counsel, protesting that he died the King's good servant, but God's first."

Many people and many causes through the centuries have looked to Thomas More as patron and hero, many have claimed him as their man. Roman Catholics claim him as their devoted churchman, and as one who died for the Catholic Church; and rightly so. Protestants, a little later in history, claim Thomas More's loyalty to conscience as a championship of what they stood for, the rights of the individual human soul. Later still, Socialists claimed Thomas More as their prophet, seeing in his Utopia a forecast of the Socialist State in which the wealth of all was shared for the good of all. New forces in human learning have again and again claimed Thomas More as their pioneer and latterly men have rightly seen him to be a prophet of Christian Unity. But greatest of all, is that aspect of him which Cardinal Heenan mentioned a week ago in the ceremony before the unveiling: Thomas More was a saint, and it is about that that I would say now a very few words.

All Christians are called to be saints. When the Apostle addresses the Christians in Corinth, a very mixed bag people indeed, he addresses them as saints, in Corinth, not because they were conspicuously saintly but because saintliness was the vocation of all of them and the principle of saintliness was already theirs through the in-dwelling Holy Spirit. All Christians are called to be saints. All Christians are saints in embryo. The Holy Spirit living in all of us is indeed the spirit of saintliness. But there have been men and women through the Christian centuries deemed to be saints because in them the spirit of saintliness did a wonderful work making them shining examples of the Christlike life in the world. And what have saints been really like? They are men and women who have been good and who have done good, but we do not naturally call everyone who is good a saint, nor do we naturally call everyone who does good a saint. What are those marks of saintliness which cause Christendom to acknowledge "here is a saint" and to want to recognise that acknowledgement sometimes by what is called canonisation. I think of two special qualities. Humility and otherworldliness: and humility and otherworldliness are qualities which not only reveal goodness and not only do good in the world, but also make the presence of God specially vivid and near and it is the mark of a saint to make God near, real and vivid to others.

First, humility. Humility does not mean a man thinking meanly about himself, rather does it mean a man forgetting himself and perhaps hardly thinking of self at all because the greatness of God is both consciously and unconsciously the supreme fact of his life. The greatness of God, the smallness of self—that is what Christian humility is about. The greatness of God our creator in whose hands we are so tiny, so tiny—almost nothing. The goodness of God as Saviour, filling a man with a sense of unworthiness because he owes all to Christ who died for him and gave himself for him. The greatness of God as judge in whose presence one day all will stand. And it is that humility in the Divine Presence, filling a whole life that is the mark of saintliness and Thomas More possessed that, growing in him through the years.

Let me quote from one of the prayers which he used in the Tower between his trial and his martyrdom.

"Good Lord, give me the grace in all my fear and agony to have recourse to that great and wonderful agony that thou my sweet Saviour hadst in the garden before Thou went to Thy bitter passion."

You see, humility. Seeing his own trial alongside the trial and the agony of Christ and thus thinking nothing of self—nothing of self, because it was the greatness of Christ's agony that meant so much to him that self was humbled, self was forgotten and it is that humility that marked him and that marks a saint of God.

Then second—otherworldliness. Those whom we call saints always have about them otherworldliness, a touch of heaven in their lives. And it means that while a saint is very much down to earth and is not less sensitive but is usually more sensitive than other people to the trials and griefs of his fellows, there is in him a kind of heavenly serenity that brings a wonderful peace and comfort to others. And the Christian otherworldliness springs from knowing that heaven is after all our goal, and the man who remembers and knows vividly enough that heaven is his goal is likely to have a bit of a touch of heaven here in his life already.

"And they who say such things show plainly that they seek a country, and if they had been mindful of that country whence they set out, they would have had opportunity to return, but now they desire a better country—that is a heavenly—wherefore God is not ashamed to be their God for he has prepared for them a city."

It is that otherworldliness bringing serenity, peace, bringing the true perspective to human life which is again and again the mark of a saint. Here I quote again Thomas More, and this time he is speaking to his singular friend Thomas Pope and as they were approaching the scaffold Thomas Pope broke down and wept and Thomas More said to him:

"Quiet yourself Master Pope and be not discomforted for I trust that we shall, once in heaven, see each other full merrily, where we shall be sure to live and love together in joyful bliss eternally."

So we salute our saint, Thomas More, in gratitude and love, Chelsea's scholar, statesman and saint; and saluting him with great gratitude and asking that we may have his prayers, that he may pray for us in heaven as he prayed so vividly in his life on earth, we remember our own calling to become saints ourselves, to become Christlike, for apart from that calling the very definition of our Christianity breaks down in vanity and paradox. And if we feel ourselves so utterly unworthy that the idea of our being called to be saints seems just ridiculous, we shall not lose heart for it is just that sense of utter unworthiness that may show that in spite of everything our feet are set upon the first of those steps that leads to Christ, to heaven.

PROFESSOR STANLEY LAWRENCE GREENSLADE

REGIUS PROFESSOR OF ECCLESIASTICAL HISTORY IN THE UNIVERSITY OF OXFORD

28 JUNE 1970

Scholar Hertford College Oxford, B.A. 1927, M.A. 1931, B.D. and D.D. 1952. F.B.A. 1960. Select Preacher University of Oxford 1938–39. Fellow and Chaplain St. John's College, Oxford 1930–43. Canon Residentiary of Durham 1943–58. Lightfoot Professor of Divinity University of Durham 1943–50. Van Mildert Professor of Divinity University of Durham 1950–58. Ely Professor of Divinity University of Cambridge and Canon Residentiary of Ely 1958–59. Fellow of Selwyn College Cambridge 1958–59. Regius Professor of Ecclesiastical History University of Oxford and Canon of Christ Church Oxford 1960–72. Select Preacher University of Cambridge 1960, University of Oxford 1961. Proctor in Convocation University of Oxford from 1964. Emeritus Student of Christ Church Oxford 1972.

17

The tenth chapter of St. Matthew's Gospel, verse 34: "Think not that I am come to send peace on the earth; I came not to send peace but a sword".

I BEGIN not from my text but from Erasmus. Erasmus was fond of talking about the Christian philosophy. Among his Colloquies is a dialogue with a young man, to whom he says that "many are frightened these days because every principle of religion is questioned". Gasper, the young man, replies: "I believe firmly what I read in the Holy Scriptures and the Creed, called the Apostles', and I don't trouble my head any further. I leave the rest to be disputed and defined by the clergy if they please; and if anything is in common use with Christians that is not repugnant to the Holy Scriptures, I obey it, that I may not offend other people".

Erasmus: "What Thales taught you that philosophy?"
Gasper: "When I was a boy I lived with John Colet. Do you know him?"
Erasmus: "Aye, as well as I know you."
Gasper: "He instructed me in these precepts."

Elsewhere Erasmus called Colet "the priest of that divine philosophy".

Plainly Erasmus does not mean philosophy, metaphysics or epistemology. "Christian philosophy", he says. "is situated in states of mind, not syllogisms; it is life, not disputation, inspiration more than erudition, transformation more than reasoning; it is rebirth". He wanted to get away (and I quote from the English version of the Enchiridion ascribed to Tyndale) "from inexplicable crooks of disputations, thorny imaginations of instances, formalities and quiddities", from Occam, Duns and their like, to something simpler. We should endeavour to make the philosophy of Christ plain to every man, he says. And so he wanted learned men who were also good men to gather the sum of Christ's philosophy out of the pure fountain of the Gospel and the Epistles, and most approved interpreters, so plainly that yet it might be learned and so briefly that it might also be plain. Christ intended to give the ordinary man a way of life, a morality based upon certain fundamental religious principles, which must not be obscured and thereby threatened, by scholastic subtleties.

113

Since these essential matters are plain enough, it should be possible, he thought, for reasonable and good-tempered men to reach agreement about them and so to maintain the unity of the Church, of the Christian community, by allowing diversity and freedom over less essential matters, as Christian charity demands. This standpoint Erasmus tried to maintain through the stormy times of the Reformation.

He saw that Colet's teaching and attitude to Scripture pointed this way. But it has been said that the true embodiment of the Christian philosophy was, for him, *Thomas More*, friend of both Colet and Erasmus. Here was the exemplary Christian humanist. He was a layman; that helped. The household of Sir Thomas More was already in his own day a manifestation of humane Christian education. As a Christian humanist More was ready to go behind the scholastics to the sources, *ad fontes*, the fountain, that is, the Scriptures, and to read them afresh, with the help of the early father of the Church whom he studied and upon whom Erasmus laboured so hard and so fruitfully. Besides this, his humanist education and outlook meant that he could write clearly, and entertainingly, speaking to the people with wit and humour. He had a satirical bent, of course, like Erasmus, and he attacked superstition and obscurantism, especially among the clergy. But this was balanced, as Erasmus himself tells us, by his extraordinary kindness and sweetness of temper. "He seems to be born and made for friendship". And behind this lay (I am still more or less quoting Erasmus) his steadfast and true piety.

Now if Erasmus and More had many characteristics and many intentions in common, there were also considerable differences which were brought out by the different circumstances of their daily lives. Erasmus was a dedicated professional scholar, working almost every day at his profession. As a scholar he was a man of peace in that he trusted (doubtless too much) the power of *education* to unite men in perception of the truth. As a theologian also, he was a man of peace, in that he thought the Church could and should maintain its unity on the basis of plain fundamentals without over-definition and heresy hunts. He was sure that Christ had come to send peace upon the earth, and by temperament he was a man of peace—except sometimes on paper, like most scholars. He was confident that his attacks on aspects of the contemporary Church would lead to reform, not disunity, and he shrank from some major decisions which perhaps he should have taken. We do not have to judge Erasmus here today.

More's daily occupation was with law and politics, in circumstances which compelled him to take decisions. He was a man of peace, too, believing, like Erasmus, in much Christian liberty. He held, and rightly so, that he should not have been forced to take some of those crucial decisions. But when he had to, he did not shrink from them. He had to experience Christ as a sword.

The first major decision was occasioned by the submission of the clergy in 1532 which meant that they renounced their right to legislate for the Church in their Convocation without the Crown's consent. More at once resigned the Chancellorship. In 1534 an Act vested the Succession to the throne in the heirs of Henry and Anne Boleyn, made it treason to slander their marriage, and ordered every subject of full age to uphold the Act by oath. John Fisher and Thomas More refused to take the oath, and they were sent to the Tower. Soon afterwards came the Act of Supremacy which declared the King to be the only supreme head in earth of the Church of England.

I shall not go into the complicated question of the legal grounds on which More was put to death, nor into the confused accounts of his trial. Enough for my purpose now to say over-simply no doubt, that he believed in the Primacy of the Pope over the whole Church as either—he was not quite sure which—as either having been provided by God, or at least instituted by the whole body of Christendom. And he concluded that the English Church could not, unilaterally, reject it, could not, as he said "without the common assent of the body depart from the common head".

I shall not discuss his opinion, which most of us here, perhaps all of us, probably don't share. I want to dwell, for a few minutes, on how amidst these pressures he handled his conscience in relation to that of others. You may remember St. Luke's version of my text and how it continues: "Think ye that I am come to give peace on the earth, I tell you nay, but rather division, for there shall be five in one house divided; three against two and two against three". Well, More's household was divided, divided in this respect against him, its head. Even his most beloved daughter, Margaret Roper, took the oath to the Act of Succession. Many of his best friends could not understand his refusal; to some it seemed an irrational scruple of conscience. Was it just obstinacy men asked? At least, let him explain his reasons: Margaret urged that.

More was condemned both for refusing the oath to the Act of Succession—that is not to the succession itself, which he said he would have accepted, but to the whole content and effect of the Act; and also for depriving the King of his title, supreme head of the Church of England. His reasons for the latter he did, in part, explain—to Thomas Cromwell, to his fellow prisoner Nicholas Wilson, to his daughter Margaret. His refusal of the oath he would not explain; the reasons were secret to himself. But both decisions bound him in conscience, a conscience which was not mere feeling but conviction after much study and prayer. Even if

115

so many other good people differed from him, "I never intend to pin my soul at another man's back", he said, "not even the best man that I know this day living". He must stand by his conscience. So then, must other men. More would not condemn them if they differed from him, provided they stood by their own consciences. But he went a step further than not condemning them: he would not meddle with their consciences.

By the time of his imprisonment at any rate he had decided not to explain, not to argue, not to try to convert others to his views. This was purely prudential so as not to exasperate the King further by those arguments, and not to endanger his own family. But it was also, for him, a decision of moral principle. He would not meddle. Let them think and pray, as he had, and come to a conscientious decision and stand by it whichever way it went. "I meddled not with the conscience of any other man that either thinketh, or saith he thinketh, contrary unto mine; but mine own conscience in this matter (I damn none other man's) is such as may well stand with mine own salvation, thereof am I, Meg, so sure as that God is in Heaven". And so, discharging his conscience, he was prepared to face the account he must give to God, trusting in His mercy.

More's respect for conscience, his courage and resolution, his trust in God, we shall all of us infinitely respect. These are truly the qualities of a saint. But there are problems in this brief story which I ought to raise and which we all might well ponder, though I can do little more than introduce them now.

When More became Lord Chancellor he was grateful to Henry for not forcing his conscience about the divorce, for employing in that matter only men who agreed with himself, and letting More and others serve him in other ways. It was a great grief to More that Henry subsequently did force men's consciences.

Now we may protest hotly against some of Henry's actual actions, particularly his actions against More himself. But they did arise out of the King's position in the State. I don't want to argue about Henry. I mean that there is a general problem about how any State, a nation, a great community holds together, about what binds it together, if that is not to be force, which we don't want. We have to prevent respect for conscience from degenerating through an improper use of the word "toleration" into a tolerance of any and every opinion, any and every action or way of life as if nothing is really better than anything else, and every one may do as he likes. That way a kingdom might stand, if we were all perfect, full of Christian charity and truth, and of commonsense: but we are far from perfect, and as we are, that way no kingdom can stand, no community cohere. What then can bind us together? What can give us a satisfying peace? Certainly More's respect was for a conscience informed by

116

principle, when a man earnestly, and if he is a Christian, prayerfully, considers the application of his principles to the immediate situation and stands by his conscientious decision. More did not stand for sheer tolerance as such, as the principle to override all other principles. It was because of his principles that he found the Oath a two-edged sword: to refuse it, he said meant the death of the body, to accept it, the death of his soul as he saw it. He preferred the death of his body.

We may be rather puzzled by his refusal to explain his reasons, but in that his attitude was limited, I suppose, to the particular issue of the Oath. I don't believe he would have generalised it to the point of saying we ought never to try to influence others. Principles do have to be taught and learned, though not without free discussion of them and, of course, with respect for conscience and individual personality. We most of us know, or if not, we must learn, how hard it can be in the human situation to reconcile the demands of truth and charity, each proper in its own right.

And so I come back to my text:—"I came not to send peace but a sword". We must take into account two Hebrew idioms which affect Jesus' manner of speech. First, "not . . . but", is not really exclusive: he doesn't mean, I don't bring peace at all, but only strife. Secondly, Hebrew religious idiom very often expresses the result as if it were the purpose. Jesus did not come *in order* to bring division, the sword. Ultimately he came to bring peace. All the same, we must not smooth the rough away, for he is not just saying: how sad it is that the peace I want to give has as a matter of fact been refused and as a matter of fact there is strife instead. He knew that the peace he offered, genuine and lasting as it is, could not come without difficulty and division. In order to bring peace he was going to do and say hard things which would bring us all to a sharp point of decision. So it is that St. John's Gospel says "My peace I give unto you, not as the world giveth", and interprets his coming in terms of judgement with a Greek word "krisis" which also means separation and decision: in fact, the crisis of decision which judges and separates, the sword upon earth. By his words, his deeds, his presence, Jesus Christ confronts us with this crisis of decision: do we or do we not accept him and his way of life; his peace, not the world's? And his peace is not soft or negative, not just letting things be in the hope that everybody will be satisfied and comfortable if he is left to his own devices. It is a positive peace, the quality of eternal life beyond history, the way to it and foretaste of it now, and also the way of genuine welfare for our society. We have been given no promise it will be an easy way—it was not so for Thomas More, and we cannot escape our responsibility either by leaving welfare to the government or simply condemning other men's ways, by saying we don't like thugs and thieves and drug-pushers and hippies or demonstrators—indeed we have to show them Christian charity. We

117

have to discover when toleration is called for, or what sort. But, above all, we have to show them that there are things, standards, principles worth caring for; that there are lives worth living, a society worth building up, a Christian philosophy. We Christians have to show that by our own care for people, our own zeal for what is true and right, by our decision for the way and peace of Christ. And so today, while we thank God for showing us that way, in Christ, and strengthening us by His grace in Christ, we thank him among all those who have given us an example of a Christian conscience at once steadfast and charitable, for Thomas More.

CANON JAMES PETER HICKINBOTHAM
PRINCIPAL OF WYCLIFFE HALL, OXFORD

4 JULY 1971

Exhibitioner of Magdalen College, Oxford, B.A. 1937, M.A. 1947. Chaplain of Wycliffe Hall, Oxford 1942–45. Vice-Principal of Wycliffe Hall 1945–50. Professor of Theology at University College of the Gold Coast 1950–54. Principal St. John's College, Durham 1954–69. Proctor in Convocation Durham 1957–70. Honorary Canon of Durham 1959–70. Principal of Wycliffe Hall from 1970.

18

The first Epistle to the Corinthians, Chapter XV, v. 19, "If in this life only we have hoped in Christ, we are of all men most pitiable.

But now hath Christ been raised from the dead, the firstfruits of them that are asleep.

For since by man came death: by man came also the resurrection of the dead.

For as in Adam all die, so also in Christ shall all be made alive."

And from v. 53:—

"For this corruptible must put on incorruption, and this mortal must put on immortality.

But when this corruptible shall have put on incorruption, and this mortal shall have put on immortality, then shall come to pass the saying that is written, death is swallowed up in victory.

O death, where is thy victory? O death, where is thy sting?

The sting of death is sin; and the power of sin is the law: but thanks be to God which giveth us the victory through our Lord Jesus Christ.

Wherefore my beloved brethren, be ye stedfast, unmoveable, always abounding in the work of the Lord, forasmuch as ye know that your labour is not in vain in the Lord."

SIR Thomas More, whom we celebrate today, was, we are told, fond of making the remark: "Man is a prisoner waiting in the condemned cell for the final moment." But I fancy he said it gaily and with a cheerful laugh rather than grimly. Because beyond death lay that glorious resurrection life with Christ of which our text speaks and in which More so deeply believed and to which he so eagerly looked forward. In his book *Utopia,* he commends the Utopians who, as he says, "although they always mourn for an illness, they never mourn for a death. They sing for joy at his funeral and lovingly commend his soul to God."

I don't think More would have been popular or fashionable today, even in Christian circles. I preached recently about death and the life to come, and an elderly and distinguished theologian said to me afterwards that it was the first sermon on this subject that he remembered hearing in years. We are, I suppose, so keen to apply our faith to this life that we are afraid that talk about heaven will encourage escapism, that it will be the opium of the people, lulling us into idle dreams about another world when we ought to be busy putting this world right. But I wonder. Could it not be that exactly the opposite is the truth? St. Paul in 1 Corinthians XV, certainly affirms that we shall make nothing worthwhile of this life unless we can see it in relation to the life to come. "If in this life only we have hoped in Christ, we are of all men most pitiable." And he goes on to give some solid reasons for this.

What the New Testament teaches, Sir Thomas More's life seems to me to illustrate. Cardinal Morton, in whose household he lived as a boy, prophesied of him "this child will prove a marvellous man." He certainly did. But I believe that much of what we find marvellous in him he owed to the fact that he saw this life in the context of the next. Let me explain what I mean.

St. Paul teaches in the Chapter from which our text is taken that Christ's resurrection is the firstfruits. "He is the firstfruits of them that are asleep." That is to say, he is the first instalment of the harvest and the pattern of what the harvest will be like. And so he shows, in his resurrection, the kind of life beyond death which the human race is to share, and indeed, the world of nature in its measure is to share. "As in Adam all die, even so in Christ shall all be made alive."

Now, the risen Christ was the same Lord who had lived on earth and died. But now he has a complete and full life. He has lost nothing. He still has his body. It's not just the immortality of the soul, a half-life going on. No, it is the whole man. But the whole man now transformed and caught up into a mode of being which is free from all the limitations of this life so his body is no longer physical, no longer liable to pain or death, no longer limited by time or space. It is a glorious whole life of completeness, a life which St. Paul compares to the new, springing, splendid stalk of grain which emerges as a result of the sowing and the dying of the one bare seed. And in this life we and our time-space world are destined to share. Indeed, this world and our life in it are the raw materials out of which God is fashioning that resurrection life of his eternal kingdom. Our world here and our lives here are the seed out of which that great harvest is to spring.

Now, how do we react if that is a true assessment of this life? Well obviously, I suggest, by getting involved. Involvement. It is a splendid world, God's world, into which he's put us and it has a still more splendid destiny. And so Christians embrace it. Certainly More did, and in two ways in particular. First, by enjoying it. He was a man who loved life, he was a happy man, noted for his gaiety. His friend Erasmus wrote of him:

"nature never framed anything gentler, sweeter, happier, than the temper of Thomas More. His whole house breathes happiness and no one enters it who is not the better for the visit."

He was devoted to wife and children, to his friends, eagerly interested in every aspect of human life. Eager in the quest of knowledge, patron of the arts, appreciative of nature, no mean theologian, a political and social philosopher as well as a man of action. He was indeed, as he has often been called, a humanist, a man who appreciated God's gift of life and the privilege of being a human being.

Secondly, he showed his involvement not only by enjoyment but by energy. This world is the raw material out of which God is making something finer still and he gives to men the privilege of co-operating, of being his fellow workers in establishing his kingdom of right and good. And so every bit of sincere service contributes to the splendour of the world to come. Accordingly More threw himself into the service of God and of the State and of his friends with all of the energy he possessed. he thought out carefully how he could best use his talents. He rejected, after consideration, the priesthood, chose the law as God's calling for him, accepted the wider opportunities which his success afforded, as diplomat and ambassador, as judge and statesman, as well as being a thinker and philosopher.

Of course he made some terrible mistakes. Persecuting the Protestants like Bilney whom he burnt and Tyndale, whose marvellous English Bible he described as a "mischievious perversion of the sacred writings intended to advance heretical opinions." And he tried to suppress the English Bible with all the machinery of the State and the rigour of the law. And his martyrdom in the Papal cause we must believe to have been the outcome of a mistaken belief, despite its patent nobility and sincerity. But though he made errors, they were the errors of a sincere Christian man, following according to his lights the highest standards of obedience to God and of service to the State and to individuals. As Lord Chancellor he administered justice without bribes or favour. As a statesman he upheld fearlessly the right as he saw it. As a thinker he strove only for the truth. God doubtless blessed and used it all, redeeming and turning to good account even the mistakes. Who can doubt that the sufferings of men like Tyndale and Bilney which he caused and the sufferings which he himself endured have all given an inspiration to generations of Christian since, which could not have been given had they enjoyed ease and worldly success.

Involvement, yes. When you see this is God's world and that you're called to help make out of it the Kingdom of God, there's no room for the view that life is trivial. Life is full of meaning and value. There's no room for the view that life is a clueless puzzle. Life becomes a splendid quest of a splendid goal.

So More found it, and so Paul tells us we should all find it. Never more so than today. "Be always abounding in the work of the Lord forasmuch as ye know that your labour is not in vain in the Lord."

Involvement is, I believe, one side of our response as Christians to seeing this world as God's world leading to an eternal Kingdom. But there is another side to that response and the two have to be held together. For the world is still only the raw material of the world to come and it is a raw material infected and penetrated with evil. It is a world of ignorance and ugliness, cruelty and pain, self-seeking and death. And that evil has to be eradicated and the material has to be shaped and developed and we are still very far from the goal. This world is never the Kingdom of heaven.

How do you react to that assessment of this life? Obviously, I suggest, if it is a true assessment, by detachment. You and I can never, as Christians, settle down in this life. We can never become at home here, we can never make this world and life in it an end in itself. If we do we shall forget the great future to which it should point us; we shall always, so to speak, live in the wilderness and never reach the promised land. Still less can we allow it to dominate us and mould us by its standards and its ways because if we do we shall no longer be the servants of God and of his Kingdom but the servants of the Mammon of unrighteousness.

The corn of wheat must fall into the earth and die if the new stalk is to grow and the great harvest is to come. And so we have to travel light in this world, and press on towards the goal. More did this and he showed his detachment as he showed his involvement, I suggest, in two ways. First, by austerity. This balanced the enjoyment. More was a humanist, but always a Christian humanist concerned with human life not as it is but as God in his goodness through Christ is going to make it. And so he disciplined himself severely. He disciplined his bodily appetites by fasting and even a hair shirt. He disciplined his use of time by giving much of it to prayer and meditation and worship. He disciplined any tendency to ambition by refusing to accept advancement until he was convinced that it was the way of service. "No one", says Erasmus, "ever struggled harder to gain admission to office than More struggled to escape it." He disciplined himself by living to a scale of values which subordinated the lesser things to the greater, the pleasures of the body to the pleasures of the mind; pleasure of all kinds to work and service; the service of the State to the service of God. He took the Chancellorship on the explicit understanding, which he stated to Henry VIII, that "I should look first unto God and after God unto him." Nor was he any facile optimist who expected and relied upon success. His own Utopians were very far from perfect. And when a friend congratulated him upon enjoying the royal favour, he remarked that he knew quite well that if the King could secure a castle in France at the cost of Thomas More's head, his head would be off that day.

And so he was ready for the acceptance of suffering and this was the second way in which he showed detachment. Acceptance of suffering balanced energy as austerity balanced enjoyment. He did, indeed, lose everything rather than renounce what he believed to be a divinely required loyalty to the Pope. Career and success. Money and goods. His family reduced to penury. He himself incarcerated in the Tower. In the end, execution and the loss of life itself.

To him this suffering and death was the journey to the fuller life, something he could accept gladly; and never in the Tower did he lose his serenity. In his cell, when his wife reminded him of the comfort and happiness of their home and begged him to compromise and be released, he replied "surely this place is near heaven too." And he could joke even as he mounted the scaffold, not inappropriately if execution was the entrance to life abundant, as he believed. "Pray for me in this life" he said a moment later, "and elsewhere I will pray for you."

Detachment. When you see that this life is a route to a more splendid world, then you can indeed practise austerity and accept suffering, because the pilgrims must go forward. There is no room here for surrender to sensuality, to self-indulgence and self-pleasing, for the rat race in search of position and money. Prosperity is no fit objective for a nation or for an individual. No room either to shrink from hardship or be shocked by pain. Comfort is not a proper aim for anyone who follows the Christian way. Life becomes a triumph through suffering gladly accepted in faith and love and hope of life to come. Paul bids us all accept that challenge; "the sting of death is sin but thanks be to God which giveth us the victory through Jesus Christ our Lord."

Involvement; enjoyment and energy. Detachment: austerity and acceptance of suffering. Could they be held together better than they were by More in his final words to his judges. "More I have not to say, my Lords, but that like as the blessed apostle St. Paul was present and consented to the death of Stephen and kept their clothes that stoned him to death, and yet be they now both twain holy saints in heaven and shall continue there friends for ever, so I verily trust and shall therefore right heartily pray that though your Lordships have now on earth been judges to my condemnation, we may yet hereafter in heaven merrily all meet together to our everlasting Salvation." Could it be put better that that? Yes, I think it could. By St. Paul.

"Thanks be to God which giveth us the victory through our Lord Jesus Christ. Therefore, my beloved brethren, be ye stedfast, unmoveable, always abounding in the work of the Lord forasmuch as ye know that your labour is not in vain in the Lord."

PREBENDARY HENRY COOPER
RECTOR OF BLOOMSBURY, LONDON

2 JULY 1972

Kelham Theological College 1929. Proctor in Convocation London from 1951. Member of the British Council of Churches from 1956, World Council of Churches from 1961. Master of the Royal Foundation of St. Katharine's 1963–68. D.Litt. Vice-Chairman Church Assembly House of Clergy from 1965. Prebendary of St. Paul's Cathedral London from 1969. Rector of St. George's Church, Bloomsbury from 1969. Secretary Archbishop's Commission on Roman Catholic Relations 1969–71. Archbishop's Adviser from 1971. Chairman, General Synod 1972–75.

19

The Gospel according to St. Luke, Chapter 22, Verse 38: "Lord", they said, "here are two swords now". He said to them (I imagine rather brusquely) "That's enough".

THROUGHOUT history there has been a tension between Church and State and the Mediaeval theory of the two swords has little to do with the text that I have taken except as a peg on which to hang the idea, but it concerns the balance between the secular and the spiritual arms. In our day, alas, that balance seems to have been made largely unnecessary by the separation of the two. But, you know, this separation could never be a permanent state of affairs as the Northern Irish situation seems to illustrate. Sooner or later in every history there is a clash either because the State claims powers which properly belong to the Church or the Church claims powers which properly belong to the State. When Our Lord was tempted to take sides over this, you remember, he asked for a denarius and then enquired whose image and name was on it. There were two parties there—the Herodians and the Pharisees. The former hoped that he might take the churchly side and so be accused of being anti-state, and the latter that he would take the anti-church side and so be discredited with the Jews, and his brilliant piece of repartee we all remember— "Render to Caesar the things which are Caesar's". That was the rebuke to the Pharisees for whom the state was all bad. "And to God the things that are God's". That was the rebuke to the Herodians, the secularists. And I dare say that there's no figure in our history who has shown a more perfect understanding and acceptance of our Lord's principle than Sir Thomas More. He certainly was no pietist like the Pharisees nor was he a secularist like the Herodians. He was a Christian humanist because he saw in the person of the Lord Christ both God and man, both spiritual and natural, a truly sacramental being. He was indeed, as he said at his death, "the King's good servant but God's first", a better citizen because a Christian and a better Christian because a devoted citizen. It is my lot to pass several times a week through the gateway of Lambeth Palace with Morton's Tower above. If you know your Hardy or happen to have visited the Dorset village which he called Kingsbere but which is properly Bere Regis, you will know of that marvellously constructed roof of the church given to his home village by Cardinal Morton, Archbishop of Canterbury. It was this Morton who built the gateway tower and in it for a

129

time lived as a page one Thomas More, son of the Judge, Sir John More, and it was here that he began his education as a courtier and it is significant that it was with the Mitre rather than with the Crown. His education as a humanist at Oxford and at Lincoln's Inn added to this. You know, despite the classical bent of the Italian Renaissance and its only faintly religious character, there was in Northern Europe nor in England no trace of the secular humanism which we know today and which we all see as the enemy of the faith as all too often it is; it was not that, it was the true humanism that he learned and shared with Colet and Erasmus, the humanism which is based upon the knowledge of *the* Human Being, Man par excellence, the Perfect Man, the Christ. Colet would later be Dean of St. Paul's and the founder of the famous schools that bear his name. These men were not mere religionists. They all saw life in a very wide spectrum and amongst More's greatest and charming characteristics is his merriness. Like some of the best monks I know he was full of fun. He would just have loved John Forrest's books of rhymes with his brother's sketches. You know, this is a Catholic trait and an Anglican trait too. You never find a Protestant making jokes about his religion or about himself but those cartoons of John Forrest exactly fit Sir Thomas More.

Merriness has a slightly different tone now but for him it expressed a deep satisfaction with the life that the Lord had given him. "God rest you merry, Gentlemen" would exactly have expressed his own attitude. It is true that some of his jokes would be considered a little crude today but they were in fact all wholesome. It is only our conventions which have changed. He was not over fond of parsons who, let it be said, were not all very admirable then any more than they are now, although he thought they were rather worse in other countries and that was part of his Englishry, no doubt. There is reason to believe that he enjoyed the Court even if later his delightful family life down the road here in Chelsea superceded it he was never a prude or a puritan. The essential point about him was that he knew the one sword from the other and never lost the proper balance between them. I will not repeat his story because you have heard it told so often on this occasion, his literary help to Henry VIII, his succession to the Chancellorship after Wolsey and the complete unsatisfactoriness of it which led him soon to resign, his refusal to commit himself on "the King's matter", the moral theological argument of the unlawfulness of Henry's marriage to Queen Catherine of Aragon despite its canonical lawfulness, his refusal to attend Anne Boleyn's coronation and the inevitable revenge that followed, and then last of all the crucial matter of the Oath of Submission acknowledging the King as supreme head of the Church which no monarch since has dared to claim. Render to God the things that are God's. And yet no man was more prepared to render to Caesar in all its fulness all that was Caesar's due. Then the long imprisonment in the Tower, the villainy of Rich, and the almost festive occasion of his beheading. Like many another who went to the Tower death was a setting free, although few could have met it so joyfully. I was called on a matter of exorcism to the Tower recently and was surprised to learn that despite all its blood-stained history and the awful things that happened on the green outside no sense of evil seems to be apparent there. There are in fact only two ghost stories and they are both of sentries, one in the 18th Century and one quite recently and both alleged that they had seen ghosts as excuses for being found away from their posts. You see, men like Sir Thomas More were essentially clean men and they died blithely. You remember what he wrote to his daughter, Margaret Roper, whose monument is in the chapel here, the day before—"I would be sorry", he said, "if it should be any longer than to-morrow. To-morrow I long to go to God. It were a day very meet and convenient for me", and then showing his intense humanity, "I never liked you manner toward me better than when you kissed me last. Pray for me, and I shall for you and for all your friends that we may merrily meet in Heaven".

It's good to remember that all those dreadful executions at the Tower of London were executions of Christian men and women who made their confessions and received their communion before they went to the block. If we had a wave of terror like that today God help the souls who had to endure it. One day we may be called upon again to stand against the State if it encroaches upon the things of God as indeed it has in many countries in our generation, but surely the chief thing that we see about St. Thomas, the thing which gave him both his merriness and his courage, was his utter faith in the God of Heaven who he hoped and believed with no shadow of doubt that he would see after death and in whom he expected to be united with all his family and with all his friends. Perhaps the saddest thing about our own contemporaries is this loss of faith. Few people to-day really believe in a future life, still less in one which is utterly merry. It is very rare that I come through the West End late on a Saturday night but I happened to do so last night and I have never seen so many thousands of people just milling about, it seemed quite aimlessly, and I reflected as I came through how many of these people have any idea at all of the God who made them and who loved them, the God who wants them to be his own for ever, wants them to share his own eternal family life. It is indeed a sad thing that in our generation the faith for the multitude seems for a time at least to have gone. Many things contribute to this: a false idea of science and its ability to answer all questions, but this is rapidly beginning to fade, a loss of confidence in the scriptures and an appalling ignorance of them, the astonishing survival of the heathen notion that we are just bodies occupied by spirits—and who on earth wants to be a disembodied spirit? A great deal of sheer evasion and an amazing capacity which our contemporaries have of just pushing things aside as though they were not there, but most of all the loss of a living relationship with Him who is the resurrection and

131

the life. You cannot read the New Testament in a detached manner, if that is possible for any of us now, without seeing that the thing that matters is faith and faith is a kind of relationship of trust with the risen Christ. No Christian wants to minimize the cross for without it there is no salvation and no answer to the nagging problem of evil, no satisfaction about sin, but taking this for granted the New Testament writers are simply obsessed with the joy of the risen Christ, with their union in Him, already in some sense sharing his risen life and looking forward to its fulness in a happy heaven, the sphere where He and all their friends are, living in amity, in fruitful communion with each other by reason of their communion with Him. Now it might be thought that a Tudor family lived very close to death and therefore to this other world beyond, and it is true that their life expectancy was far shorter than ours, much the same as that in India today. It is true that courtiers were in constant jeopardy of a tyrant's frown, it is true that disease had few antidotes in that unscientific age, but there were no wars comparable with the two through which we have lived, there were no aeroplane crashes or train disasters and there was nothing like the decimating horror of the motor car on the roads. We do in fact live as close to death as they did, perhaps closer, and in any case whether we do or not, our little life is soon to end, whether 10 or 50 or more years on. There is every sign today that the long reign of materialism and unspirituality, of mere rationalism and affluence in property and pleasure is coming to an end and great numbers of people are turning to spiritual things, not, alas, yet to Christian things, although a few are, but many are turning to demonic things, many to Eastern religions, many to spiritism and the host of agnostic sects which are as popular today as when the Church first faced the heathen world in the 1st Century and made such amazing progress. Men are seeking the unknown God as in Athens when St. Paul preached in the Agora and was invited to the Areopagus. Then as now the crucial doctrine was the resurrection. Paul made so much of it that the Greeks thought he was preaching about a new goddess called Anastasia, Resurrection, and I suggest to you that if you would honour Chelsea's greatest resident and know the joy of Christian fellowship that he knew and knows, if you would gain his courage and his blithe acceptance of an end to a lesser life in exchange for a greater and a better life, if you would share with him the high blessedness of bearing witness in such a way that others are uplifted and strengthened, if you would in short be as true and as Christian as he, then you must begin again to think of your life here as a risen life, of your baptism as having united you to the risen Jesus, of your future as being right merry with him in the family life of heaven where your Father as well as your Elder Brother live and with them in the communion of their common Holy Spirit the vast company of the children of God, More and Roper, Katharine, and no doubt a penitent Henry and Anne, our own forbears, and relatives and friends, all in happy satisfaction

132

and sweet content. Yet this eternal fellowship is not an overwhelming confusion for in a strange way that we cannot yet grasp, just as Heaven is free of the time we know and of the space we know, so number also is brought into manageable proportion by the universal mind which is God the Word and which we will share with Him. Christians do not think enough about death because they do not think enough about Heaven. Death is unmentionable to most of our contemporaries but death to the saints is a birthday and its sequel a marriage breakfast. The greatest saints, or at least those who are near enough to us to let us understand them like Francis and Teresa, share with Sir Thomas More this blessed joy in God, his utopia and his household—to quote Erasmus "of delightful fellowship", where all the members of the household find occupation, no strife occurs, no cross word is uttered but discipline is maintained by courtesy and benevolence. These are foretastes of what he looked and hoped for and now enjoys. He and all his learned to know their divine host here in Chelsea and when he passed over on Tower Green or when his beloved Meg died in her bed some years later they were not abashed to pass over because they already knew and loved the same Host of the Heavenly Land. So let us praise God for this happy saint and pray that we may both share now and when we die, and that may be any day, the resurrection glory of his Lord and ours.

CANON JOHN COMPTON DICKINSON

SENIOR LECTURER IN THEOLOGY IN THE UNIVERSITY OF BIRMINGHAM

8 JULY 1973

Exhibitioner Keble College Oxford, B.A. 1934, M.A. 1938, B.Litt. 1938. F.R.Hist.S. 1942. F.S.A. 1947. Fellow Emmanuel College Cambridge 1947–50. Select Preacher University of Cambridge 1950–58. Fellow and Chaplain of Pembroke College Cambridge 1950–60. Select Preacher University of Oxford 1957–59. Lecturer in Theology University of Birmingham 1960–62: Senior Lecturer from 1962–73.

20

" "THAT your joy may be full". If one were to seek to put into half a dozen words the whole purpose of Christ's giving us his full revelation of God, one could not find any half dozen words better than that. That is what religion is about; it is about joy. When Sir Thomas More was canonised, when other saints are canonised in the Roman Catholic Church, one of the qualifications which they very rightly insist on at headquarters is a supernatural joy. You cannot be a Saint, you cannot be a Christian, unless you are joyful.

I remember hearing Archbishop Temple once say: "There is no greater heresy than the idea that Christianity is dull." And, doubtless, you and I here all know people—practising Christian folk of one kind or another—whose character we specially admire for it is dominated by that quiet, sustained joy. You see it, don't you, in mothers of large Christian families. Mothers who very often have to do a lot of work and very often have not got the money they want, but they are at peace with God. They have joy in their vocation. I've seen it as a priest in enclosed communities of nuns, both Anglican and Roman Catholic. The thing that strikes you most is the joy that radiates from them.

And so it is with the great saints. St. Francis and those that followed him were, above all, joyful people. And if you look at the correspondence of Sir Thomas More, the thing that strikes you is his astounding capacity for joy, or, as often he puts it, for "being merry". We find him joyful in all seasons. When the sun was shining or when the thunder clouds were looming very black overhead. For example, when he heard of the loss of barns of corn, which at that period constituted a very heavy financial blow, he wrote to his wife: "I pray you with my children and your household, be merry in God". And when he got a letter from a son that pleased him greatly, it wasn't just the diligence and the ability behind the composition of the letter that he liked, but as he wrote, he liked it because "he playeth pleasantly with me and returneth my jests again very wittily". And so he went on. You may remember when he was summoned into that legal trap that was to effect his imprisonment and death, he returned here to Chelsea, and it was noted of him that he was "very merry". Knowing that he had been in this very great crisis one asked him "Sir, I trust that all is well because you are so merry?", though all was far from well—at least in the eyes of the world. Again, when the shadow of death had got very

135

near indeed and he was imprisoned in the Tower, Mary Roper visited him and, we are told, after they had said Psalms and the Litany, he was ready to sit and talk and "be merry".

And so one could go on. Surely this matter of joy is worth considering in this present age. Industrial society may have increased our economic and social standards, but one scarcely can say it has increased our merriness. How many tight-lipped, anxious, tensed-up people one sees when one goes to any great town in Western Europe. Why was Sir Thomas More apt to go through life with the sensible soul-based merriness of the saint? There were I think two reasons. First of all he did so enjoy to the full the world that God had made, made by the God who was good. His was not a one-track mind.

How boring quite good people can become if they have one-track minds. I think of university colleagues who can only talk about their research, of the type of clergyman who can only talk about his parish, of the type of mother who can only talk about her family. Sir Thomas More never got into that sort of rut. He was, of course, perhaps the greatest lawyer of his age. And one can sense that he enjoyed being a lawyer. He enjoyed the exercise it gave to his immense gifts—his capacious memory, his ready wit, his dispassionate, incorrupt judgment, his profound humanity. And he did enjoy writing, especially, I suspect, that intriguing work, *Utopia*. He must have enjoyed, being what he was, writing that plea for the poor, urging that the authorities stop hanging so many people for theft and get down to the problem of abolishing the poverty that caused the theft. And surely he must have had an impish delight when he wrote there of the people of his Republic that they utterly exclude and banish the whole race of lawyers—not a common sentiment among Lord Chancellors.

And then he enjoyed all that new learning that was flooding into England from Italy, and which had become the great rage. The learning in which he excelled so greatly. So much so that Erasmus (perhaps the greatest intellectual of Western Europe at the time) saw that More could have attained stupendous success if he'd gone on as a don. And he enjoyed singing in the choir here in Chelsea with people well below his social level, even if it shocked some at a time when social distinctions were very much alive. And I suspect, though I can't prove it, that if he lived today he might well have joined some of his social inferiors to give vocal support to Chelsea's attractive soccer team.

The entire joy he took in his family, that is too well-known to require stress. Yes, he is rejoicing in things. But notice, secondly, that though he rejoiced he never gave things more than unconditional allegiance. If he rejoiced, he was also to some extent suspicious, a little afraid, careful to

136

see that he did not give them an allegiance which would be unfruitful for his eyes were, after all, perenially fixed on the City that is eternal, the "City not made with hands"—the City of God.

It is difficult, isn't it, to love a thing and to distrust it simultaneously? It's difficult psychologically, to some extent difficult theologically. And again and again, Christians of all kinds, Catholic or Protestant, have failed in that. It's fairly easy if you've a strong sense of the call of God to despise the world. The world is evil. The Desert Fathers thought that, and you can find Puritans in England, rather too many of them, at various periods who were equally suspicious of things in the world. Drink was wrong, sex was wrong, Roman Catholics were wrong. That sort of thing. Yes, it is easy to do that. And it's easy also to do the other thing. To take the gay superficial view that everything in the world is going along very well. "God's in his Heaven, all's right with the world." That is a great fallacy beloved of English people more than most fallacies. It was, of course, dominant in the 18th Century. And the trouble about it, of course, was that it just was not true. All's right in the world! That was all right if you were a duke or a duchess, living in an elegant country home with beautiful furniture and silver and pictures of the period, and enormous staffs of domestic servants working all hours at something rather less than cut rates. But, if you were one of the domestic servants or if you were one of those Africans who at that time we carted like cattle to become slaves in the New World (sometimes thrown overboard like cattle if the weather was rough and the ship looked like sinking) then you did, after all, find it pretty difficult to believe that "all is right in the world". And so it was that although More loved deeply, he loved as it were conditionally, watchfully, one might almost say suspiciously. None loved his wife and children more than More, but that did not mean that he idolised the married state as such. He performed that difficult balance which we in the Church of England find especially difficult to maintain, between love of married life and love of the monastic life. This loving father, this loving husband, always entertained the most profound admiration for the monastic life, even in its most conservative form, that of the Carthusians. And its value, its fascination was always with him— happily as his marriage was.

That intellectual brilliance which Erasmus admired, would have made it possible for him to have gone on to become a famous don, corresponding with the highbrows of Western Europe. But because of his spiritual depth and width he saw that the intellect alone is inadequate to bring a man to God.

It was here again, that suspicion, that distrust. Then what about that legal life? How easily he could have been a highly successful lawyer making great sums of money getting on with all the right people. But law for him was just one activity, an activity which could be dangerous, could be defective. He never sold his soul to that.

So also with money. At one period I read abstracts, no small number of letters and papers of the reign of Henry VIII. When one reads those papers, papers of all sorts of people, one cannot fail to be struck by the profound wave of greed, of avarice, which crept over England at that time. The sort of avarice of which we see so much today, for it was one of those ages when money was made the great idol. And yet, look at More. There is very little sign that he had any special interest in money as such. He would enjoy the things it gave, but he was never being enslaved by them and that is why he was merry.

How did he achieve this detachment which bred full enjoyment? That is the final question we ask. It's been rightly said of More that he took to himself the best of the old Catholicism of the Middle Ages and fused it with the best of the Italian Renaissance that was now paramount.

The Middle Ages, despite obvious defects in its piety, saw that our life is something we must regulate with a constant sense of death being in view, of death and judgment. Victorian Protestants and Medieval Catholics too often spoke of judgment, hell-fire and so forth in a crude way which theologians today would not be ready to accept. But if we get rid of the crudities that still does not alter the fact that you and I were not only made by God and called by God, but that we will be judged by God. We cannot be at one with Him unless we are taking seriously the task of making ourselves, if not God-like, at least God-worthy. And behind all More's secular activities and interests, behind all his fascination that he found in activities, there lay, and you haven't got to go far to see it, this very profound, persistent, disciplined piety. His cheerfulness and strength did not come from mere will-power. Surely, if anything is certain, it is that will-power is never strong enough by itself. More, one could say, soaked himself in the supernatural, so that he was living with one foot in Heaven long before his cruel death. There was his passionate, unbroken devotion to the Sacrament of the Body and Blood of Christ. His regular use of the invigorating spiritual cold shower which we know as the sacrament of penance. That and other standard devotions of the time. And it was noted that he never took a major decision without careful prayer; that he was regular in his worship.

No few modern men have broken their moorings and so are apt to think that something that is not new is not true. But the experience of church worship down the centuries has, as it were, hammered out things which are perennial, and if those sort of Christian disciplines and graces still go on it is because they have been found so satisfying that they have not been needed to be replaced. Surely this disciplined devotion is something we must not under-estimate here. Medieval Catholicism with all its faults is psychologically sound in insisting that your will and my will is something which must be hammered into shape, into God's shape, week after week, month after month, year after year, because it is only by that sort of process that we build up that supernatural strength which can make us merry. No room either to shrink from hardship or be shocked by pain. Ease is not a proper aim for anyone who follows the Christian way. Life becomes a triumph through suffering, gladly accepted in faith and love and hope.

Involvement, humanism and merriness. Detachment, austerity and suffering. Could they combine to produce more impressive utterance than More's final words to his judges? "More I have not to say, my Lords, but like as the blessed apostle Paul was present and consented to the death of Stephen and kept their clothes that stoned him to death, and yet be they now both twain holy saints in heaven and shall continue there friends forever. So I verily trust, and shall therefore right heartily pray, that though your Lordships have now here on earth been judges to my condemnation, we may yet hereafter in Heaven merrily meet together to our everlasting salvation".

PROFESSOR JOHN McMANNERS

REGIUS PROFESSOR OF ECCLESIASTICAL HISTORY IN THE UNIVERSITY OF OXFORD

30 JUNE 1974

St. Edmund Hall, Oxford, B.A. 1939, M.A. 1945. Chaplain and Lecturer in History of Politics at St. Edmunds Hall, Oxford 1948–56. Fellow 1949–56, Dean 1951–56. Professor of History University of Tasmania 1956–59, University of Sydney 1959–67, University of Leicester 1967–72. Regius Professor of Ecclesiastical History University of Oxford from 1972. Canon of Christ Church from 1972.

21

The 24th verse of the 1st chapter of St. Paul's Epistle to the Colossians: "Who now rejoice in my sufferings for you, and fill up that which is lacking of the afflictions of Christ in my flesh, for his body's sake which is the Church".

TODAY we commemorate a great Englishman and a patriotic citizen of London, Sir Thomas More, who died beneath the axe of the public executioner on the 6th July 1535, because he refused to yield to authority on a question of moral principle. We pray for him, as we pray for all the faithful departed, and as we hope our fellow Christians who come after us will pray for us too. We pray for him and we admire him. We reflect on his Christian greatness and we resolve to do what we can to follow his Christian example. We pray that we may be strengthened in our endeavours to do so.

Essentially the Christian is a follower of Jesus Christ and there could be no greater or finer example. But Jesus with His great mission, His sinless life, His intense spiritual insight, His overwhelming singleness of purpose, is so far beyond us that we need other examples—examples nearer to us, nearer to us in our family life, in our ordinary work, in our games, in our frivolities, and, it must be confessed, nearer to us in our sins and in our failures. We need lives like our own, but on a higher plane, for our examples, and from these we can learn much, and such an example is Thomas More.

He thought of becoming a priest and if he had done so he would have had a great career before him. The son of a successful London lawyer, a youth trained in the household of Archbishop Morton at Lambeth, and above all having been educated at the University of Oxford, an intelligent young man with scholarly tastes, he could have hoped to rise high in the ecclesiastical profession, and in that age going into the Church was very much a professional business. It was a career. But More tested himself, according to his friend Erasmus he went about this with the utmost seriousness. Erasmus writes, "He turned towards the religious life by watching, fasting, prayer and similar tests, preparing himself for the priesthood, more wisely than the many who rush blindly into that arduous calling without first making trial of themselves". And then, adds Erasmus,

141

he discovered that the celibate life wouldn't do for him. "And he had almost embraced this ministry but as he found he could not overcome his desire for a wife he decided to be a faithful husband rather than an unfaithful priest".

But notice the sequel. More is not one of these all or nothing Christians, he is not one of these young men who think very seriously about ordination and decide against it, no doubt rightly, and then are rarely seen around the Church, or at most just as a worshipping Christian. No, More discovered that there was a layman's vocation within the Church as demanding as that of a priest. And here is a lesson for all of us. Do not think because ordination is not for you that this means that there is no special vocation for you in the Church, a vocation to be more than a worshipping Christian—a vocation to leadership.

Anyhow, More decided he couldn't be ordained, but this didn't mean he chose a life of cheerful worldliness as a layman. As a layman he lived a very sober, regulated life, more sober than that of many of the clergy of his time. He lived simply. He wouldn't indulge in the fashionable sport of gambling. At penitential seasons he wore a hair shirt (I do not of course recommend this practice). And in the share-out of family chores his daughter Margaret had the special responsibility of washing it. And he prayed continually. His friend Erasmus said, "He prays at set hours and he prays from the heart". And in that house out in the countryside at Chelsea there were prayers morning and evening for all the members of his numerous family and all the servants, and Scripture reading at mealtimes. We do well to consider this example of the devotion and piety of a bygone age. Now I don't suppose that most of us, the fashion being what it is now, could persuade our families to join in common prayers or Bible reading over meals. My two younger children who are still at home, and my two elder ones who I'm glad to say come back frequently at weekends, would be astonished if I proposed such a thing. But fashions change. And remember that even so, whatever the fashion today, the foundation of the Christian life is prayer. And in this matter there is no separation between clergy and laity.

Prayer then is one of the great characteristics of More's private life, and marks him as a true Christian. And another characteristic of his private life was an intense devotion to his family. Now again, as in prayer, the fashions and customs of past ages are not as our's. The highly individualistic and romantic ideal of falling in love that we accept, (or at least we accept it in novels, plays, films), this idea is a comparatively recent phenomenon in history. But Christian devotion and selflessness and caring have been exercised just as surely in the arranged marriages and despotically paternal households of the past as in the romantic love affairs and egalitarian families of the 20th Century. Erasmus tells us that More chose his wife (of course, from the appropriate propertied family—that was the fashion of the time), deliberately as someone young and untrained, "so that he might more readily mould her to his liking". he had her taught literature and "trained her in every kind of music". Another contemporary says that More really preferred the second daughter of the Colt family but he married the eldest lest she should feel slighted, which is not romantic but shows delicacy. And when after seven years of marriage his first wife died, More married again, within a month of her death. The second wife, a widow with a rich dowry, was a half dozen years older than he was, and Erasmus says the motive was to have someone to care for the children, "more for the care of his children than for his own pleasure". So there was perhaps a lack of sentimentality there in More's two marriages, but they were Christian marriages and very happy ones. As you all know, the epitaph he composed for his first companion included them both. "The second wife", he says, "a rare distinction in a helpmate, was as affectionate as if the children were her own. It is hard to say whether the first lived more beloved than the second does now. Oh how blessed if faith and religion had permitted us all three to live together. I pray the tomb and heaven may unite us, that death will give what life could not".

More was a family man, a Christian family man, and his great house at Chelsea was full of children, his own children, step-children, adopted children, and of course, in due course, grandchildren. He loved young people. He saw to their schooling. He jested with them. And as the manner of the times was he ruled them strictly too. He was one of those Christians whose Christianity showed especially in the gift for friendship. Friend of scholars, statesmen, lawyers and simple folk, and also the very young. And the secret was, I think, he had a sense of humour and he was humble. (If you find you don't get on with people, if you find that as a Christian your life is constricted by not being able to fit, ask yourself whether you have those two things. A sense of humour, of course one can't always cultivate that, but are you humble?) When the great Duke of Norfolk came to see More he was astonished to hear that More, a knight risen to the lofty dignity of Lord Chancellor of England, was singing in the parish choir. "God's body, my Lord Chancellor, a parish clerk!" Actually being humble is a good way to enjoy yourself too. More was humble. I suppose he was an ambitious man, or at least he rose high in the service of King Henry VIII. He went on diplomatic missions abroad. He became Chancellor of the Duchy of Lancaster, High Steward of the University of Cambridge, and finally in 1529, on the fall of Cardinal Wolsey, Lord Chancellor. At first he had refused preferment seeing that serving the King might bring him into conflict with his beloved city of London. When finally he did accept advancement from Henry VIII he had no illusions about the savage, fickle nature of the master he served. Henry would come to visit More at Chelsea and this was very flattering, "But", said the Lord Chancellor, "if my head could win him a castle in France it should not fail to go".

Well I don't know if he was fundamentally ambitious or not, but whether he was or not the point is this: Very often, not perhaps always, but very often, a Christian has a positive duty to accept high office and great dignity, and great responsibility. There is no more dangerous myth than that the Christian life consists in withdrawal from the world. Or indeed that Christian life consists in being in the world but remaining in the background, that Christians are essentially quiet backroom boys. A Christian's duty is to serve the world and to lead it as required. The Christian's duty is involvement. Whether you are ambitious or not seems to me not to matter much. Your duty is involvement. And involvement is a tragic business. It must be tragic for there are problems in the world in which no course of action is entirely right or just, or even approximately so. In the Middle East, say, or in Northern Ireland, whatever course of action is taken is unjust. Whatever course of action is taken is going to cost lives, is going to be tragic. But there can be no hope of a settlement, there can be no hope of peace, unless someone accepts heavy responsibilities and makes intolerable decisions. And so More accepted involvement in the cruel and treacherous world of Tudor politics. It was his Christian duty and it destoyed him.

One of the early Fathers said, "The Kingdom of Heaven is not necessarily confined to fools!" Perhaps it could be put a little more closely into our modern idiom by saying "not necessarily confined to bores". Our Christianity should make us into fuller personalities. Christianity should extend our interests and our sympathies, should encourage us into new fields of endeavour, make us more enterprising and cheerful. And More certainly, with all his political involvement, was a full man, a rich, lively, interesting personality, a man of many accomplishments. A busy lawyer, a statesman, a student of Greek, who worked at the education of his children, including the girls on the same footing as the boys, which was unusual for that day. In his spare time he wrote history. An unfinished study of the reign of Richard III is for its time a masterpiece. In severe moments he wrote works of religious controversy—Alas for his memory, one might say, for the progress of Christian standards has left him revealed as, in the last resort, a man of intolerance. And he could write, at least in his younger days, knock-about comic verse. Indeed the knock-about is literally so, in his poem *A Merry Jest—How a Sergeant would learn how to play the friar*—for the sergeant, the constable as it were, disguised himself as a friar to arrest a debtor but found that friars were even more unpopular than sergeants, and he got thrown downstairs and beaten up by the wife and servant. "They roll and rumble, and turn and tumble as pigs do in a poke". Not perhaps highly sophisticated modern T.V. humour, but not bad for a young man with academic and political ambitions. And above all, as everybody knows, More wrote that splendid book *Utopia,* a work of satire, a proclamation of reform, an essay in what I suppose today we would call science fiction. The Utopia was a Christian work in that it bitterly criticised the social abuses of the day, directly or by contrast with the fabled country it describes— it attacked grasping landlords, monopolists, the excessively harsh criminal laws, useless expenditure on luxury. Now of course, fine book as it is and Christian book as it is, I don't say one would have wished to live in More's Utopia. It was a Communist state with some totalitarian elements. There were no fashions allowed in clothes, so I suppose young ladies would not wish to be there. Foreign policy was nationalistic and cynical. When a young man I would have objected to the compulsory lectures before breakfast; growing older, I have qualms about their enthusiasm for euthanasia. But one mustn't take this science fiction dream world too seriously. The serious part is the moral criticism of social evils and the rest, very much, I'm sure, a Jeu d'esprit. The world is still wracked with social evils. Under-developed countries overseas, under privileged people at home, forces, ruthless forces, striving for mastery, striving for economic prominence. There are all sorts of social evils still with us. And we might say to ourselves "What can I do about all this as an individual?" Well of course you can't do much. We feel helpless, but be assured there is something you can do, at least indirectly. More wasn't free to act against social evils. He was a servant of the Tudor absolutism. But he had a witty pen and a flowing Latin style and he wrote, in a disguised form, a complaint against social injustice which has been remembered ever since through many generations. We may not wield effective pens but we all have our circle of conversational influence. We all have our milieu where our opinions count for something. And do we make it known how we stand as Christians in matters of injustice to our fellow men? Does anybody know how I voted in the last election? Did I argue with anybody about what policies should be? Did I let people know what I thought? Do I ever say anything about injustices to be put right? Or do I feel as a Christian that the thing to do is to slink away and not express an opinion? I don't believe Christianity demands meek people who just vote and don't say anything. Public opinion rules and in the end I suppose public opinion is built up by the sum of innumerable private opinions. We ought not to keep silent. Within our limitations of ability, within the proper due performance of our duties, acting within our status, we ought to be interested citizens, helping to form the climate of opinion.

If a man speaks his mind on burning contemporary questions, if he accepts high office in the state, if he assumes a role of leadership in the community, he must take seriously the possibility that his opinions and policies may be mistaken. A Christian ought to be open to the conviction of error. He ought to be tolerant, not attempting to force or manoeuvre other people out of their own beliefs. "I beseech you", Oliver Cromwell once said to religious zealots, "I beseech you in the bowels of Jesus Christ to think it possible that you may be mistaken". And here comes the ultimate tragedy of Christian involvement in the world. Involvement is our duty. It may drive us to the tragic necessity of taking decisions in which either course is cruel. But worse still, involvement means that in the end, in spite of prayer, in spite of sincere reflection, we may be mistaken. Sir Thomas More with all his zeal, his friendliness, his understanding, was, so far as religion was concerned, an intolerant man. Europe was stirring with new religious ideas and ideals, with demands for the reform of the Church, demands for independence from the corrupt court of Rome, with proposals for the suppression of superstitious doctrine, with schemes for making the Scripture accessible to all in the common tongue, and More had little sympathy with all this. He denounced the pestilential sect of Luther and Tyndale. He denounced the translation of the New Testament, taking the view that the better the translation it was, the more dangerous. He defended the monasteries against proposals for reform, drastic ones it is true. Heresy he believed should be rooted out by force; it was a carbuncle, he said, which should be clean cut out to prevent further infection. His own summary of Book Four of his *Dialogue Concerning Heresy* runs like this. "The author sheweth his opinion concerning the burning of heretics and that it is lawful, necessary and well done. And sheweth also that the clergy doth not procure it but only the good and politic provisions of the temporality". Of course this was a common opinion of the time, but if we are to talk of More as a Christian example the common opinion of the age is no excuse. Burning people for their religious opinions, the charred flesh, the cracking bone, is said to be "necessary and well done" and "good and politic". Let us be frank, it is not possible to say anything more deeply and outrageously unchristian.

Nor should we assume, because of Sir Thomas More's heroic death, that the cause for which he died was justified thereby, or at least you should carefully define the cause for which he died. The majority of Englishmen, the majority of honest English Christians did not agree with him. They wanted their Church reformed. They wanted it freed from the corruption of Rome. They saw no alternative to royal leadership. They saw no peace, no safety from renewed civil war but in the assuring of the succession to the heirs of Henry and Anne Boleyn. More's closest friends did not share his scruples. Indeed with a more civilised king on the throne, More's life would not have been forfeited, for More himself was willing to grant pretty well everything that was significantly at issue. He would accept the succession to the throne. He would agree that the Pope was inferior to a General Council. He would remain silent on the question of the King's new title, the Supreme Head on Earth of the Church of England. But in the end when the ruthless king—and to be fair to him he was beset with fears and dangers—when the ruthless king demanded More's complete submission, he would not take the oath to the succession in the form to which it was tendered to him. It was a narrowly poised decision and that makes his courage all the more astonishing. Think of the circumstances. All England virtually is obedient to the king. More is being made an example of in company with a mere handful of people, Bishop Fisher and half a dozen monks. He was facing death over a form of words and over an issue that branded him as failing in his patriotic duty. Though in the end he was beheaded he didn't know the king would allow a merciful end. The standard penalty for treason was hanging, drawing and quartering, all done slowly. He had counted the cost before he risked his life. To his daughter Margaret he wrote, "I forgot not in this matter the counsel of Christ in the Gospel that ere I should begin to build the castle for the safeguard of my own soul I should sit and reckon what the charge would be. I counted, Margaret, full surely, many a restless night while my wife slept what peril was to fall to me and in thinking I had a full heavy heart". And in prison in the Tower More thought of Christ at Gethsemane. He said "Let us conform our wills to His, not desiring to be brought into peril of persecution, for it seemeth a proud high mind to desire martyrdom, but desiring the help and strength of God if he suffer us to come to the stress. In our fear let us remember Christ's fearful agony, that Himself would for our comfort suffer before His passion, to the intent that no fear should make us despair. And let us ever call for His help". He thought of Christ's agony in the garden before the Crucifixion. Let us remember this message of Sir Thomas More when the time comes for us to suffer.

St. Paul says in Colossians in the words of our text that he rejoices at his own suffering because, a daring thought, it fills up what is lacking in the sufferings of Jesus. Jesus has not suffered enough. The nails and the spear were not enough agony. Others must suffer with him too. And as the shadow of death crept nearer to the frail and ageing prisoner in the Tower, the presence of Jesus became clearer before his eyes. And so to his daughter Margaret he wrote astonishingly of joy. "Good daughter, never trouble thy mind for anything that ever shall happen to me in this world. Nothing can come but what God will. And my good child I pray you dearly be you and all your sisters and my sons too comfortable and serviceable to your good mother, my wife, and I right heartily pray both you and them to serve God and to be merry and rejoice with Him. And if anything happen to me that you would be loth, pray to God for me and trouble not yourself, as I shall full dearly pray for us all that we shall meet together in heaven where we shall be merry for ever and never have trouble again".

And when death came, More showed no fear and he refused to dramatise himself. His last words were to the executioner. "I pray you let me lay my beard over the block"—lest he should cut it. So he departed this world with levity. His last words were not of his family, which he loved, not of the great matters concerning Church and King, but of his beard. In God's other kingdom they will meet again, those adversaries who fought each other for their opposing views of the Church. They will meet and be reconciled—Cramner who was burned, More who was beheaded. May we learn from the history of their bitterness to be tolerant, always to think it possible that we may be mistaken. May we learn from the intensity of their belief what a serious duty we have to serve our Master, and may we pray that we too may meet with them in God's other Kingdom "where we shall be merry for ever and never have trouble again".

CELT

THE REVEREND LEONARD WALLACE COWIE

SENIOR LECTURER IN HISTORY AT WHITELANDS COLLEGE, LONDON

29 JUNE 1975

Exhibitioner Pembroke College Oxford, B.A. 1941, M.A. 1946. Peterhouse Cambridge Diploma in Education 1942. University of London M.A. 1948, Ph.D. 1954. Chaplain and Tutor College of St. Mark and St. John Chelsea 1945–47: Tutor 1947–68. Whitelands College, Putney from 1968.

22

" AND seeing you have at Chelsea a right fair house, your library, your books, your gallery, your garden, your orchard and all other necessaries about you where you might in the company of me, your wife, your children and household, be merry, I muse what in God's name you mean here still thus fondly to tarry".

This was the way—according to his son in law William Roper—in which Sir Thomas More was bluntly saluted by his wife Dame Alice, when she visited him in 1534, during his imprisonment in the Tower of London. Now I can hardly take these words as my text this morning but I have quoted them at the beginning because I propose to talk about his house in Chelsea, his household and his family and above all else, his attempt to establish it as a Christian community in Chelsea.

More seems to have gone to Chelsea in about 1518 when he was some forty years old: a master of requests, a favourite of Henry VIII, a friend of scholars and the author of *Utopia* which he had written some three years earlier. Born in Milk Street, educated at St. Anthony's School in Thread-needle Street and trained in law at the Inns of Court, he had, except for his years at Oxford, lived most of his time in the City. He was one of the first Londoners to seek a rural retreat in middle age, though his reasons for doing so were not completely such as have inspired his later successors. As a young man More was attracted by the monastic life; while a law student he lived for about four years in the London Charterhouse, probably in one of the houses it had on its property which lodged unmarried laymen. There, according to Erasmus, he devoted himself, though without taking vows, to the vigils, fasts and prayers and similar austerities of the Carthusians. From this time he began to wear "a sharp shirt of hair next to his skin which he never left off wholly" and flogged himself frequently with a whip of knotted cords and restricted his hours of sleep to four or five a night.

The Carthusians of course didn't lead a typical monastic existence: they were vowed to silence, each lived in his own cell within the monastery, working and devoting several hours daily to mental prayer, and they only met each other for the daily office and the communal mass and ate together only on feast days. More was probably drawn to them because they were an exception to the decline among monastic houses at

151

this time, but their individualistic, withdrawn existence didn't appeal to him and it is said that when for a time he thought of taking vows it was as a Franciscan friar and not a Carthusian monk. In the event, however, he decided upon marriage and a family instead of the monastic life. He married in 1505 and during each of the next three years had a daughter: Margaret, Elizabeth and Cecily, and finally in 1510 a son, John. His wife died in 1511 and within a month he married his redoubtable second wife who cared for his motherless children. He began his married life at a house called "The Barge" in Bucklersbury and his children were born there. But soon after his second marriage he moved to "Crosby Place" in Bishopsgate Street Without, which was a larger town house, and the hall of it was of course to be transferred in this century to a site close to where his Chelsea house once stood.

As might be expected, More shared the concern of many thoughtful, religious men of his time with the problem of adapting the limited ideal of the mediaeval cloistered life to the wider possibilities of everyday Christian life, and at Crosby Place he began his attempts to achieve this in his own household. He himself often rose at two o'clock in the morning for religious contemplation and study. Though he didn't care for ball games he took part in family jokes, music and charades or plays, but he didn't consider dice or cards proper recreation, and even when his children were young they weren't allowed to play at them. His personal appearance caused him little concern and he never encouraged the children to take much interest in clothes or fashion. Nor did he care for elaborately cooked food or strong drink, preferring milk and fruit and eggs with small beer or water to choice meats and wines. As his daughters grew up, however, he evidently had to temper such monastic severity and abstemiousness to feminine weakness, for in a letter he later wrote to them contained a reminder that he had fed them with fruit and cakes, given them pretty silken dresses and if ever he had to punish them had beaten them only with a rod made of peacock's feathers so as not to injure their tender skin.

Utopia was written towards the end of his years in Crosby Place: though most of the book describes contemporary England, the brief account of the imaginary kingdom which is little more than an appended parable, is the best known part. The outline of Utopia, a fictitious island set in recently explored seas, was suggested by the discoveries of the Portugese and Spaniards. It is set forth as an ideal, though not a Christian community; Utopians, like monks and friars, may possess nothing, must wear the common habit, their hours of work and recreation, their very pastimes, which may not include foolish and pernicious games such as dice, are regulated. They eat in refectories beginning every dinner and supper by reading something relating to virtue and good manners; discussion at table is initiated and directed by the older people who graciously encourage the younger married couples to join the talk by making it a sort of oral examination. Men below the age of twenty-two and girls below eighteen serve or else stand by in marvellous silence listening to the conversation of their elders as they eat. Discipline in the kingdom is rigidly enforced: the penalty for breaking its law is bondage or if need be, death. Family discipline in Utopia is equally strict, the conception is patriarchical; "their women when they grow up are married out but all the males, both children and grandchildren, live still in the same house in great obedience to their common parent", and it is clearly stated that "the oldest man of every family . . . is its governor" and that "wives serve their husbands and children their parents and always the younger serves the elder". Such subordination and service is secured by the traditional means of domestic punishment; "husbands have power to correct their wives and parents to chastise their children". Utopia is thus represented as an ideal community living according to natural law and practising an ideal religion; it is influenced by Plato's Republic and laws but essentially expresses monastic ideas: the common life founded on religion, the contemplative and intellectual pursuits and the respect accorded to manual occupations. High-minded, honest and humorous, but also narrow and oppressive, intolerant and puritanical. It was written by More when he was in his later thirties, some ten years after he had ended his experience of monastic life and entered upon matrimony.

Utopia shared also with monastic communities its isolation from the world, since it was an island, and More probably felt that by now he could direct his own household more successfully if he moved it from the City into the country. So conveniently approachable from London, especially by the Thames, Chelsea was until the later eighteenth century a riverside village much on its own and considered a particularly healthy location. In 1664 it had 300 acres of arable fields out of a total of 630 acres, a further 120 acres consisting of pastureland and most of the rest being meadow, common land and gardens. As late as 1705 it was estimated that the parish had no more than 300 houses and six years later Dean Swift, who stayed several times in Chelsea for the benefit of the air, wrote from there in his Journal to Stella: "About our town we are mowing already and making hay and it smells so sweet as we walk through the flowery meads".

The house More built in Chelsea, the great house, stood halfway along the Beaufort Street of today, just west of the village and east of the original farmhouse which he bought and not so near to the village. Little is known about the house itself: Erasmus called it "a modest yet commodius mansion," and Hayward "not mean nor invidiously grand but comfortable". Two plans however in the Salisbury archives at Hatfield House seem to represent the arrangement of the ground floor and first floor during More's time. They depict it as having a symmetrical front elevation with a square Tudor porch in the centre flanked by slightly projecting bays. There was a little chapel with a room above it which had an open floor so that those in it could share in the services. And this plan can be supplemented by the excellent view drawn by Leonard Knight and engraved by Johannes Kyp in 1699 of Beaufort House, as More's house was then called. This show it as renovated by Sir Robert Cecil, afterwards Lord Salisbury, who took possession of it in 1597. Despite the changes made in it by then it remained in plan and character substantially as when More built it, though it presumably originally had the flat roof from which More watched the river. It was approached by two garden courts guarded by two gatehouses and in the tree lined river front was the quay where More's barge waited to take him to Westminster. Kyp's view also shows the rural setting of the house surrounded by great acres of cultivated land; the house itself had grounds extending as far north as the present Kings Road which included an orchard and a spacious garden sloping down about 100 yards to the Thames, which had a delightful view across to the Surrey side. Waterfowl lived among the reeds and in the river itself were salmon and trout, eels and pike, carp, roach and other fish. Ellis Hayward, the Jesuit, in *Il Morro* which he wrote in 1556, a fictitious dialogue representing More's conversations with learned men of the time, described the grounds in a few words: "In them was a small hillock worth ascending for from one part almost the whole of the noble City of London was visible and from another the beautiful Thames with green meadows and wooded hills all around and the garden was crowned with an almost perpetual verdure and had flowering shrubs and branches of fruit trees that grew near interwoven in a manner so beautiful that it seemed like a living tapestry worked by nature herself". This description suggests that the garden was less formal in arrangement than in 1699.

Much more is known, however, about the life of the household in Chelsea under More's direction and as Maurice Addams has said, somewhat romantically, "Utopia was but the author's home writ large; its beautiful house on the riverside at Chelsea was through his delight in social life and music and through the wit and merriment of his nature, a dwelling of joy and mirth as well as of study and thought". By now his family was growing up: Margaret married in 1521, Elizabeth and Cecily in 1525 and John in 1529. Unlike Utopian wives, his married daughters and their husbands stayed with their parents and lived in the great house together with his son and his wife, eleven grandchildren and Margaret Griggs, an adopted relative. Such a large community was naturally self-contained in its activities; More was not the lord of the manor though he shared the manorial privilege of a chapel in this church. He sang in the choir "with a surplice on his back", shocking the Duke of Norfolk: "God's body, my

Lord Chancellor, a parish clerk!" Otherwise the contacts of the household with the outside world seemed to have come mainly from the many visitors who visited More: Hans Holbein who had been introduced to him by Erasmus, painted the well known picture of the family here in 1528 and is said to have stayed three years in Chelsea. Other visitors include Colet, Grocyn, Erasmus, Archbishop Wareham, Bishop Fisher and Henry VIII, of whom Roper recorded: "For the pleasure he took in his company would His Grace [the King] suddenly sometimes come home to his house at Chelsea to be merry with him, whether on a time unlooked for he came to dinner and after dinner in a fair garden of his walked with him by the space of an hour holding his arm about his neck". It is from the accounts of some of these visitors that we are familiar with life in the great house in Chelsea. Erasmus, in one of his epistles, emphasised the aspect that appealed most to a religious scholar, "In More's house you would say that Plato's academy was revived again, only whereas in the academy the discussion turned upon geometry and the power of numbers, the house at Chelsea is a veritable school of Christian religion; there is never seen any idle, the head of the house governs it not by a lofty carriage and oft rebukes but by gentleness and amiable manners". Erasmus approved also of the way in which all the members of the family were employed: "If you should hear them playing skilfully on various instruments of music or watch them pouring over every kind of Latin or Greek author like busy bees . . . you would say they were muses toying sweetly in the loveliest parts of Ionica".

There was some relief from such Renaissance earnestness. Gardening was also encouraged as an activity and More was mediaeval enough to keep a fool. But in general he continued to impose his desire for monastic austerity upon the household, including the servants for whom he seemed determined to deny not only participation in unwholesome pleasures but also the pleasures of matrimony into which the members of his family had entered: playing dice, cards and all games were of course forbidden to all men and women and so too was flirtation. Indeed the sexes were strictly segregated, men and women servants living on opposite sides of the house and seldom even speaking to each other, though their constant attendance at domestic prayers was required. Regular prayer and worship inevitably had an important place in the life of the community. When More was at home he continued his custom of rising at two in the morning and spent five hours in study and devotion, after which he took private prayers with his children and said "the seven Psalms, Litany and Suffrages following" with the whole community. Similarly "so was his guise nightly before he went to bed, with his wife, children and household to go to his chapel and there upon his knees ordinary to say certain Psalms and Collects with them": the three Psalms: Have mercy on me, O God",

"To Thee O God have I lifted up my soul" and "May God have mercy on us"; the Hail, Holy Queen with its prayer, and finally "Out of the depths" for the dead. he also heard mass every morning and on Sundays and festivals everyone had to go to church and on great festivals rise to attend the Midnight Office. Similarly the meals took place at Chelsea in an atmosphere of monastic devotion: at the table "a passage of sacred Scripture was read with the commentaries of Nicolas of Lyra or some other ancient writer" by one of his daughters or very often Margaret Griggs. The passage of Scripture was "intoned in the ecclesiastical or monastic fashion" and was concluded with the words "And do Thou O Lord have mercy on us" as in monasteries and nunneries. The reading was continued until More gave a sign for it to finish and then he would ask one of the company how this or that passage should be understood.

At some distance from the great house More, "because he was desirous for godly purposes sometimes to be solitary and sequester himself from worldly company", erected the New Building of which no trace now remains. It contained a chapel, a library and a gallery and there on Fridays usually continued he from morning until evening, spending his time only in devout prayers and spiritual exercises, while each year on Good Friday he assembled the whole household there to hear the whole of Our Lord's Passion read, generally by John Harris, his secretary. "Thus delighted he evermore", wrote Roper of his father in law, "not only in virtuous exercises to be occupied himself but also to exhort his wife, children and household to embrace and follow the same".

The death knell of the community at Chelsea came on the April morning in 1534 when More left the great house for the last time, entered Roper's boat from his garden gate and was rowed down the river to Lambeth Palace to appear before the Royal Commissioners who were to tender the oath of succession to him. After his execution the house passed to several successive owners, including the great Lord Burleigh, and finally to Sir Hans Sloane who demolished it in 1740. Today some fragments of walls and windows at the back of Paultons Square and the southern end of the Moravian burial ground are said to be parts of the original building, surviving as the only outward remains of the community which ceased to exist in the age when Martin Luther violently rejected the monastic ideals which it sought to preserve and extend. And there we must leave the house and the community and yet we might perhaps remind ourselves that these ruins together with the ruined abbeys and the site of the manor house of Little Gidding in England and the memories of Calvin's Geneva and the Pilgrim Fathers' New Plymouth in Massachusetts, that these ruins in Chelsea speak of the continual attempt in

156

history of men and women to establish ideal communities wholly given to the practice of Christian life and worship, an attempt which still continues and is likely to continue as long as the Christian religion is practised and endures.

THE RIGHT REVEREND ALAN CHARLES CLARK

ROMAN CATHOLIC BISHOP OF EAST ANGLIA

18 JULY 1976

Priest 1945. Doctorate in Theology, Gregor-
ian University of Rome 1948. Tutor in
Philosophy, English College Rome 1948–53.
Vice-Rector 1954–64. Auxiliary Bishop of
Northampton 1969–76. Titular Bishop of
Elmham 1969–76. *Peritus* at Second Vatican
Council 1962–65. Joint Chairman Anglican-
Roman Catholic International Commission
from 1969. Roman Catholic Bishop of East
Anglia from 1976.

23

"Our Lord keep me continually true, faithful, and plain." The words of Thomas More writing to Margaret.

ANYONE, my brethren, who has been invited to preach this annual sermon, must have felt it a great privilege, and I feel it perhaps more than anyone who has preceded me. I feel again the sense of thrill and excitement that I had some years ago when I preached in the Cathedral of Rochester, the Cathedral of John Fisher. And I imagine that our patron, Thomas More, scholar, statesman, saint, is listening with us today to see what this ultimate preacher might have have to add to what must have been, indeed, has been, a wealth of scholarship, of wit and of doctrine spoken by others from this pulpit.

I can make no such claim. All I can claim is to share with you a great love of Thomas More—and love is a unity. It is, therefore, in a spirit of great unity that I would like to reflect with you on some aspects of this great and wondrous man.

Driving yesterday down from Norwich, on the long haul to South-ampton, one had a great opportunity to think on him and to wonder about his reactions to some of our attitudes and presumptions today; whether it be in our law and customs, in our home life, or in our priorities. For he had a great love of life, of human life, a great love of his age, and of the immense criss-cross of thought and of emotion and of adventure that characterised it. And I would like to reflect briefly on the changing attitude in Thomas, especially in his attitude to death, as he suffered, a victim of tyranny, and never changed his course but went forward in it ever more adventurously.

I feel strongly that his attitude to death has a lot to say to us, for, strangely, in the goodness of God, in death we have a unity irrespective of our provenance. Thomas was unsure of his ability to meet death, with his convictions upheld and with no weakening; and in this he speaks to all of us weak and feeble people. You will remember how he looked upon the Carthusians from Charterhouse, going with great firmness to their deaths, and he wondered whether he could do the same, or whether he would not yield under torture—as we would well wonder the same. He had no doubt

159

that these Charterhouse monks would stand firm, for, he said, their whole life had been built up for this moment; and he mused whether *his* life really led to the moment which he could foresee quite clearly before him. Therefore, no doubt with you, I love that prayer of his: "O Lord, keep me continually true, faithful and plain." That wonderful word "plain".

Thinking on it, does not one come to the conclusion that he meant single-eyed, unambiguous—not just integrity but clarity of purpose; not swayed by doubts or fears, but just to go ahead, plain, without pretension. For Thomas had no pretensions about himself, which is why his common humanity floods into our weakened, strained humanity. When in our legislation, or whatever, we seem to be tampering with the human and throwing aside the traditional convictions of this nation about life and its sanctity, we are accommodating a passing lack of confidence in ourselves. It is strange that in moments of lack of confidence legislation accumulates. Thomas knew his law, he knew the rights of his people, he knew the rights of the poor. He was quite severe with the disturber of the peace, and, going to his dreamworld of Utopia, it is strange to meet the severity of some of the legal penalties. But one thing he demanded of his Utopians was that they should rejoice and be merry when one of them died. Therefore, one can perceive a great continuity between that early philosophical, speculative position and his own position in this very spot some years later.

He believed—and his Utopians were told to believe—in a great communion of saints. That those who died were with those who remained and there was converse between them. And he lived out this conviction, so much so that one can say to him today: Thomas, you are among us, listening and, no doubt, correcting the prose and wondering whither will go the theme, and whether the preacher has really seen his sense of the meaning of death. With temerity, I think one has.

He says: "Give me the grace, good Lord"—as we have heard—"to set the world at naught." And goes on: "I beseech God, give me and keep me the mind to long to be out of this world and to be with him." I think he has seen the enigma, the basic enigma, of the Christian faith, that it would be very strange to profess that faith and not long to meet God; and there seems in the latter months of his life a great flooding of grace whereby he literally longed to see God. And if we do not have that longing, then one of our unities is missing. Do you, do I, long to see God and set this world at naught? Or are we busy building great secure bonds, setting up a mortgage on our future? A Christian should long to see God. And Thomas—again reflecting on this—knew his sins, his waywardness, and all the things we find so hard to perceive in him but would give him no accolade if we denied they were there, for he says so—says (and here I love him): "For I can never but trust that who so long to be with him shall be welcome to him. He that so loveth him that he longeth to go to him, my heart cannot give me but that he shall be welcome; or were it so he should come ere he were well purged."

Thomas creates a space for everybody who longs to see God, who longs to be with God, even though sin, evildoing and mistrust may crowd in, and realised much more than his contemporaries that this longing is two-way—for God, too, longs to be with man. "Trust shall I God", he says, "to enter in a while his haven of Heaven, sure and uniform."

Sure and uniform—how he parallels the plainness he asked God to keep in him. And then in those final days as he prepared for death, he puts into the mouth of Christ words you know well, yet words on which, I feel, we should continually reflect. He makes Christ speak to him: Pluck up thy courage, faint-heart, though thou be fearful, sorry and weary and standest in great dread of most painful torments; be of good comfort, for I myself have vanquished the whole world, yet felt I far more fear, sorrow and weariness and much more inward anguish too when I considered my most bitter painful Passion to press so fast upon me. But thou now, O timorous and weak silly sheep, think it sufficient for thee only to walk after me, which am thy shepherd and governor, and so mistrust thyself and put thy trust in me. Take hold on the hem of my garment therefore, from thence thou shalt perceive such strength and relief to proceed.

So Thomas More was geared for his death, a man who loved life.

Today in our society, in our country which we love, there is hostility to life along with a longing to live it more abundantly. The awful ambiguity of man, that he strives to have a life on his own conditions and according to his own construction; that he strives to have a life which does not square with the revelation of what is human given us in Christ. Then by statute or legislation or by choice or by attitude he ultimately becomes hostile to life. And if my generation, which is shared by some of you, cannot show more love of life, then the succeeding generation, which is with us already, will cast us out and rightly so. And hence our legislation and statutes, in keeping with the justice promoted by Thomas More, should give the priority to life. Yes, there are problems; yes, there are balances to be kept—and one has not wit and trusts so much in others to do this, and rightly so. But the priority must be on life and the only way we can preserve and further and mature the life of the nation is individually to long to be with God.

There is the riddle, the enigma, which makes the good news of the Gospel utterly strange and alien in some respects to human thought. But there is between us here today in this historic church a unity, and your

161

gracious Vicar, when he welcomed me and gave me my origins, spoke of a work for unity to which I am committed with all my heart. But I find as the years progress that we must seek unity at every level, at every level of human life—and it is unity in our attitude to life as promoted and preached without preaching by Thomas More that we think of in this commemoration service.

We love him, we feel with him and we know that he was indeed a great Englishman. But he was God's, and so at the end when Meg hugged and kissed him for the last time, it is not strange to find him unmoved, for the choice had already been made and all the future was clear before him, and he knew that in the great communion of saints he would be with her and with us for all time. But he will constantly demand of us the willingness to choose eternal life begun here rather than a world-centred life, however good, however generous. And if we do this, then the rest is given us a hundredfold—all the humanum, the human, is given back to us, enriched, strengthened, loving and tender. And looking on Thomas we see it etched on his face: intensely human because intensely Christian.

So as a final thought, let us all strive to have the justice of More, the dream of More, and the plainness of More, so that we will never be guilty of the double talk that destroys man and destroys human relationships. And let each of us, striving to find our unities, build on every one we find, and the strangest of all is that in death, which after all is made precious by being inserted in the death of Christ, we find the unity which More found on the scaffold.

SIR THOMAS MORE
OUR MOST ILLUSTRIOUS PARISHIONER
BORN 1478

THE REVEREND GEORGE IAN FALCONER THOMSON

DIRECTOR OF THE BIBLE READING FELLOWSHIP

26 JUNE 1977

Balliol College, Oxford. B.A. 1934, M.A. 1938. Chaplain Hertford College Oxford 1937–46. Junior Dean and Dean of Degrees 1939–42. Chaplain Oxford Pastorate 1938–42. Secretary of General Ordination Examination 1946–52. Chaplain and Senior Lecturer St. Paul's College Cheltenham 1962–66. Director of the Bible Reading Fellowship 1968–77.

A new ring of bells was installed in the belfry of Chelsea Old Church and dedicated on 4 December 1977. The tenor bell is inscribed: "Sir Thomas More. Our most illustrious parishioner. Born 1478". The first full peal was rung to mark the Quincentenary of More's birth.

24

"Render to Caesar the things that are Caesar's;
and unto God the things that are God's." St. Matthew 22: 21

OUR purpose this morning is to honour the momory of Thomas
More, man of the world and man of God, and this we will do in
the context of this church (where he worshipped) and its symbol-
ism.

As you walk from the West door to the East end of almost any church
you pass through the nave, then into the choir, and up to the chancel or
sanctuary. The nave is the body of the church, holding an earthly
congregation and representative of our earthly life. The choir, singing to
the glory of God, reminds us of angelic hosts, and the inevitable transition
from earth to heaven. The sanctuary betokens the throne of grace where
sins are forgiven, life is restored, and we are united in the peace and love
of God. Thus is the Church meant to be our guide through life, a spiritual
power-house, and our preparation for fellowship with God.

Thomas More's life was a progress through these three stages.

We think of him worshipping in this very place, a dedicated layman,
illustrious and renowned, yet humble and humorous, one with everyone
else in the practice of his faith. For three years he had thought of being
ordained, which is not surprising. At the age of 13 he had been a page at
Lambeth Palace, where the Archbishop of Canterbury, Cardinal Morton,
became his patron. He then went to Oxford, but only for two years, and
not long enough to collect a degree. He was already a marked man in
character, spirit and intellect, attractive and able. When More was only
twenty-one Erasmus wrote to a friend in a letter dated December 5th, 1499,

"Whenever did Nature mould a character more gentle, endearing
and happy, than Thomas More's?"

But he remained a layman. He went to the Inns of Court, New Inn,
Lincoln's Inn, and Furnival's Inn. He became a Member of Parliament at
26, Under Sheriff of the City of London, an Envoy to Flanders, Privy
Councillor, Speaker of the House of Commons, Chancellor of the Duchy
of Lancaster, and, of course, Lord Chancellor—after Wolsey—filling 28

165

years of public life with notable service. What a man to have as a regular worshipper in this congregation.

This is not to forget his leisure moments, when he was frequently a favourite at court; when he wrote and published his *Utopia;* when he was a match for any intellectual, including his monarch, whom he entertained in Chelsea. Typical that at the Field of the Cloth of Gold, when the Kings of France and England were trying to outstrip each other in regal splendour Thomas More preferred to sit in a tent and chat away in academic conversation with the great Greek scholar Budaeus.

There is not much More hadn't done or couldn't do, if required, in loyalty to King, country, office, family, or general duty. That was all in the nave, so to speak, his worldly life, his successes, achievements and high distinction.

But deep in his nature was a strong religious instinct, which overrode all other concerns. He rendered to Caesar the things that were Caesar's, without neglecting that deeper loyalty which is to conscience, truth, and faith. He found strength in prayer, joy in his worship, and wisdom in the Divine revelation. He relished the pattern of life which grew out of the discipline, dogma and pietism of Catholicism, and nothing would bend his will on these matters. He resisted the intrusion of Reformation doctrines and interpretation. He hunted and hounded those who challenged the teachings of Catholicism; and all who threatened or infringed the rights or authority of the Papacy were anathema to him. Tudor absolutism and the whims of his own sovereign eventually fell into this category, and he saw no alternative but resistance. The tension between right and wrong, between what he held dear to God and what he saw as acceptable, these tensions became acute, and gradually led to a shedding of earthly cares, or sitting more loosely upon them, in favour of personal and spiritual integrity. He moved from the nave to the choir, to join the voices that led the worship, an indication of the priority of spiritual matters over temporal, and the nurturing of his own soul against the day of reckoning. Even when he was Lord Chancellor he enjoyed singing in the choir, and described himself as a "clerk", in the chorister sense.

His wife, Jane Colt, bore him three daughters, Margaret, Cicely and Elizabeth, and an only son John. When she died he built that tomb, between the choir and the sancuary, up in the chancel, and we can imagine him happy in that part of the church which gave him such joy. He married again, and looked forward to the day when he and both his wives would lie content in the same tomb in this church, a day which never came.

Then came the penultimate crisis when Thomas More was forced by circumstances to choose between his King and the Pope, the lawful Head of the Church, as he saw the Pope, and the usurper of ecclesiastical authority, as he saw the King, In 1532, one day only after Convocation accepted the royal supremacy, More resigned as Lord Chancellor, and returned to private life. We can picture him enjoying his family, his house, his garden and this church, whence he drew strength for the indignity to come.

He was taken to the Tower on 17th April 1534, where without complaint he settled down to meditate and write. For the previous eleven years (1532 to 1534) he had been engaged in controversy with Reformation leaders, including Tyndale, and was busy attacking what he regarded as heresy both at home and overseas. he rightly saw the advance of Protestantism as a serious challenge to Catholicism, and was unsympathetic to any national upsurge against Papal claims, whether in England or in Europe.

There is always a danger that we may sentimentalise or romanticise Thomas More, and forget the intensity of the issues at stake at a critical period in English history. Henry VIII's marriage problems tend to steal the limelight from more fundamental matters that touched the national life at the sensitive points of religious faith and obedience, and intellectual freedom. This was precisely where the division between duty to Caesar and duty to God was complicated and precarious, as it was in the context of our text. Our Lord balanced it perfectly without in the least detracting from the irremovable intrinsic tension.

Once in prison Thomas More's mind turned to the need to comfort and reassure his own family, rather than attack heresies on the continent and at home.

So he wrote a *Dialogue of Comfort,* which has been described as "a severe meditation by one who has come to terms with his lot, and is able to tell others how they can win spiritual comfort in any troubles that may arise." His imprisonment was initially for life and involved the possible loss of goods. Nothing his second wife could do could persuade him to change his attitude, plead for clemency, and perhaps return home. All he had to do was to take the Oath of Supremacy, but this would have meant the surrender of his deep-seated Catholic conviction. He refused to give way.

Thomas proceeded to write on: *A Treatise on the Passion, Treatise to Receive the Blessed Body of the Lord,* and *Certain Devout Meditations.* He wrote, for example, the sentence: "What worse offence could be imagined than to despair of God's help, and by running away to hand over to the enemy the battle-station which God had assigned you to guard."

He was in prison for nearly fifteen months, and during the last month was deprived of all books, paper and pens. Imagine the desolation of having nothing to read, no means of recording anything, and no way of communication, especially for one who had been at the centre of the nation's life. He must have guessed what was in store for him, and was beheaded on July 6th, 1535, at the age of 57. So had he moved from the nave to the choir and to execution, or, if you prefer, from this Church into history and back again, into this series of commemorative sermons.

Next year will be the quincentenary of Thomas More's birth on February 6th, and it seems appropriate to devote a few moments to the significant changes that have happened in the relations between the Roman Catholic Church and the Anglican Communion in the last few years.

Since the Vicar of Chelsea Old Church inaugurated these sermons in 1954 the estrangement that hardened in Thomas More's own lifetime has been remarkably eased, and in some dramatic ways bridged. Archbishop Geoffrey Fisher's visit to the Pope, John XXIII, in 1960, notable and historic, broke the fixation of isolation. The Vatican Council of 1963–65 publicly acknowledged and documented the "special place" of the Anglican Communion in relation to Rome. The visit of Archbishop Michael Ramsey to Pope Paul VI in 1966 evoked a further easement, and prepared the way for an International Commission of Anglican and Roman Catholic theologians to see how far "convergence" can be reached on such fundamental doctrines as the Eucharist, the Ministry, and Authority in the Church. This has all been done in the last six years, an Agreed Statement on the Eucharist (Windsor 1971), the Ministry (Canterbury 1973) and on Authority (Venice 1976). Had Henry VIII and Thomas More been members of this Commission they would probably have been impressed by the depth of fellowship, scholarship and good sense that pervaded the deliberations. Surely we may attribute this to the action of the Holy Spirit upon the will and insight of the Commission members.

It is, therefore, in the wake of these three Agreed Statements that the present Archbishop of Canterbury, Dr. Coggan, paid his recent visit to the Vatican, and on the 29th April this year (1977) he and the Pope, Paul VI, both signed a Common Declaration, which contains a vital and challenging sentence:
"The moment will shortly come when the respective Authorities must evaluate the conclusions."

Surely it is fair to add the hope that instead of Archbishops of Canterbury always going to Rome some future Pope may pay a reciprocal visit to Lambeth or Canterbury as a gesture, and proof, of genuine good faith and cooperation.

Like many an Anglican over past years I too have had my reservations about the invocation of saints, excessive Mariolatry, and the doctrine of infallibility. But we have all moved together in recent years to the safer shores of the Bible, the Creeds, the early Councils, and the Sacraments, and in these deep harbours find safer anchorage. Negotiations and mutual recognition are on a more realistic and contemporary basis, and are charged with rather less unyielding prejudice. After all Thomas More himself had a direct descendant in Elizabeth's rein (Elizabeth I) who was a good Anglican clergyman. It is, therefore, fitting that we should thank God for the new spirit of understanding that has accrued in recent years, and pray that it may lead to fuller agreement and cooperation in the years ahead.

Above all, let us pray that the God whom we all serve, the Father of our Lord Jesus Christ, may bind us all together in a single peace, as we in this Church pledge ourselves anew to
Render unto Caesar the things that Caesar's,
and unto God the things that are God's.

THE LORD ARCHBISHOP OF CANTERBURY THE MOST REVEREND AND RIGHT HONOURABLE FREDERICK DONALD COGGAN, D.D.

PRIMATE OF ALL ENGLAND AND METROPOLITAN

5 FEB 1978

Scholar St. John's College Cambridge, B.A. 1931, M.A. 1935. Hon. Fellow 1961. Wycliffe College, Toronto, B.D. 1941, D.D. 1944. Professor of New Testament, Wycliffe College, Toronto 1937–44. Principal, London College of Divinity 1944–56. Macneil Professor of Biblical Exegesis London College of Divinity 1952–56. Consecrated Lord Bishop of Bradford 1956. Translated to York, Archbishop, Primate of England and Metropolitan 1961. Chaplain and Sub-Prelate Order of St. John of Jerusalem 1966–67. Prelate from 1967. Select Preacher University of Oxford 1960–61. Translated to Canterbury, Archbishop, Primate of All England and Metropolitan, 1974. F.K.C. 1975.

The major exhibition at the National Portrait Gallery entitled, 'The King's Good Servant—Sir Thomas More 1477/78–1535' involved international co-operation and aroused world-wide interest. The exhibition was held from 25 November 1977 to 12 March 1978 and was organised by Richard Ormond, Deputy Keeper, and designed by

Michael Haynes. Outstanding works of art were lent to the exhibition including the famous drawings by Holbein of More and his family from Windsor Castle, the copy of More's own prayer book with his annotations (Yale University), and the portraits of Erasmus and Peter Gillis by Quentin Massys which they sent to More as an expression of friendship. The great libraries of Europe lent books, manuscripts, letters and documents written by More and his contemporaries, and, among nearly 300 items, were many of superb quality and unique significance. The 148 page illustrated catalogue was produced by Professor J. B. Trapp, Director of the Warburg Institute and Professor H. Schulte Herbrüggen of Düsseldorf University.

MORE TOMB

Translation of the Inscription, from Thomas Faulkner's
History of Chelsea, 1810.

Thomas More, born in the city of London, of an honourable though not illustrious family, was yet very conversant in literature; who after he had for some years, while young, pleaded in the courts, and acted as judge in the sheriff's court in the city, was summoned to Court by the invincible King Henry VIII to whom alone of all kings, the unheard-of glory happened to be stiled Defender of the Faith, which honour he merited both by his pen and his sword, was chosen of the Council, knighted, and at first appointed Vice-Treasurer, then Chancellor of the Duchy of Lancaster, and at length, by the great favour of his sovereign, Chancellor of England. But previously he had been elected Speaker of the House of Commons, had several times been sent on embassys; and lastly, in the embassy to Cambray, was joined as colleague and companion with Cuthbert Tunstall, at that time Bishop of London, but since of Durham, than whom the world has scarcely a more learned, prudent, or virtuous man. There he was present as an embassador, and saw, with joy, leagues renewed, and peace, so long desired in the world, restored among the greatest monarchs of the Christian world.

'Which peace may Heaven confirm, and render lasting.'

While he was thus employed in a course of honourable duties, so that neither the best of princes could disapprove his labours, nor was he

171

odious to the nobility, or disliked by the people, only feared by thieves, murderers

His father, Sir John More, Knight, advanced by his sovereign to the rank of a Justice of the King's Bench; a man, courteous, gentle, blameless, mild, merciful, just, and upright, aged, indeed, but active in body, having his life prolonged to see his son Chancellor of England, conceiving himself to have stayed long enough on earth, willingly departed to heaven. But the son, after his death, (to whom compared when alive he was called the young man, and seemed so to himself), missing his absent father, and weighing in his mind that he had four children and eleven grandchildren, began to grow old; a bad state of health succeeding, another sign of old age, increased this opinion: therefore sated with mortal affairs, that which from his infancy he had prayed for, in his latter days to be at liberty, withdrawing himself by degrees from the cares and business of this life, to meditate on immortality; that (if God should favour his endeavours) he obtained on resigning his honours, through the incomparable favour of his prince; and he caused the tomb to be erected for himself, having bought hither the remains of his first wife, that it might admonish him daily of his approaching death. Good Reader, I beseech thee that thy pious prayers may attend him while living, and follow him while dead; that he may not have done this in vain, nor trembling may dread the approach of death, but willingly for Christ's sake undergo it; and that death to him may not be altogether death, but a door of everlasting life.

Sir Thomas More's first loving wife lies here;
For Alice and myself this tomb I rear.
By Joan I had three daughters and one son
Before my prime or vig'rous strength was gone.
To them such love was by Alice shown
In stepmothers, a virtue rarely known,
The world believed the children were her own.
Such is Alicia, such Joanna was,
It's hard to judge which was the happier choice;
If Piety or Fate our prayers could grant,
To join us three, we should no blessings want.
One grave shall hold us, yet in heaven we'll live,
And Death grants that which Life could never give.

25

"Join the struggle in defence of the faith, the faith which God entrusted to his people once and for all." Jude 3, N.E.B.
"Let us cease judging one another, but rather make this simple judgement, that no obstacle or stumbling-block be placed in a brother's way." Romans 14, 13 N.E.B.

THERE is little need to re-tell the story of the life and work of Thomas More in such a place as this, nor to such a congregation as this. Most of us, probably, have seen that fine play *A Man for All Seasons.* And most of us have seen the splendid More Exhibition now on view at the National Portrait Gallery. We may consider ourselves fortunate if we are the possessors of the Exhibition catalogue which bears all the marks of careful scholarship and skilled presentation.

Anyone who lives at Lambeth Palace, as I do, must think with pleasure of the fact that More, at the age of thirteen, was a page-boy to the Archbishop of Canterbury, John Morton, after whom part of that building is named. With some prescience and insight, Morton wrote of the boy: "He is a merry lad who will become a marvellous man". Both adjectives, "merry" and "marvellous", could well be used to describe Thomas when he came to maturity. Anyone who has Canterbury in his diocese, as I have, must be allowed at least to mention the fact that, if Chelsea Old Church has the body of More, Canterbury has his head— safely buried in the Roper vault in St. Dunstan's Church in our city.

Tomorrow is the five hundredth anniversary of this great man's birth, and we do well to meet together to remember him in the presence of God. In his person, and in this place, we have a special meeting point between Anglicans and Roman Catholics.

173

As you entered the church this evening, you probably paused to look at the statue—"Sir Thomas More, scholar, statesman, saint"—erected in 1969 in his honour. If you did not, you will doubtless do so on your way home. It would be an interesting exercise, if you felt so inclined, to follow the river as far as the Victoria Embankment Gardens and there to look at another statue, itself a memorial to another great man, a contemporary of More's, William Tyndale. For long he has been a hero of mine, and when I pass his statue I feel moved to stop and do his memory reverence.

Let me very briefly sketch the characters (without re-telling the biographies) of the two men as I see them.

Thomas More's mind was made in the mould of a scholar, He rejoiced in the company of men of letters. When he was a young man of twenty-one, he met Erasmus, and they became life-long friends. John Colet—there is a name still revered in the City of London!—William Grocyn, William Lily, William Latimer, Thomas Linacre—what a galaxy of close friends! They brought to him all the riches of the Renaissance, of the beauty that was Greece and the glory that was Rome. They stimulated the thinking and the writing of one another, and their influence can be seen in the Latin orations which More used to make at official receptions. His learning was seasoned with wit and the undoubted prolixity of his writings, and especially of his controversial works, was relieved by a delightful sense of humour.

He moved with ease in Court circles, and was greatly appreciated there. But, if we are to judge by the fine picture of More in the company of his father, his household and his descendants (by Rowland Lockey, after Holbein), he was happiest of all in his family circle where all the younger members, girls equally with boys, shared in the culture, the wit and the affection of a man of affairs and of deep religious conviction. His religion had under-girded him all his days—in his youth he thought seriously of entering the contemplative life—and at the end sustained him during fifteen months in the Tower and to the last when he laid his head upon the block. It says much for the calibre of the man, for his intellect and for his culture, that Erasmus, on hearing of More's death, said: "I feel as if I had died with More, so closely were our two souls united".

At home with the Bible, with the Fathers, and with the classics, More's was a well-stored mind. But it is in his prayers that one can often see deepest and most clearly into the soul of a man. We listen, not only with pleasure to the linguistic beauty of this prayer composed during his time in the Tower, but with reverence to the note of a deep religion in the heart of the writer:—

174

"Good Lord, give me the grace so to spend my life, that when the day of my death shall come, though I feel pain in my body, I may feel comfort in my soul; and with faithful hope of thy mercy, in due love towards thee and charity towards the world, I may, through thy grace, part hence into thy glory."

William Tyndale's was one of those "deathless minds which leave . . . a path of light"; there is no one whose effect on the growth of the English Bible is comparable to his. Because of the influence which his translation had on the Authorised Version—something between seventy and ninety per cent of that version is pure Tyndale—he can well claim to have enriched our language more than Shakespeare or Bunyan. What drove him on in his work was his passion to make the principles of the Bible available for all to learn. "If God spare my life", he remarked to an ignorant divine in Gloucestershire, "ere many years I will cause a boy that driveth the plough shall know more of the Scriptures than thou dost". He, like More, was influenced by men like Erasmus and Colet. His heart would have warmed to the words that Erasmus wrote in the *Exhortation* with which he prefaced his New Testament of 1516: "I totally dissent from those who are unwilling that the sacred Scriptures, translated in the vulgar tongue, should be read by private individuals. I would wish even all women to read the Gospel, and the Epistles of St. Paul. I wish they were translated into all languages of the people. I wish that the husbandman might sing parts of them at his plough, and the weaver at his shuttle, and that the traveller might beguile with their narration the weariness of his way."

So strongly did this passion burn in Tyndale that he was content to spend the last twelve years of his life (1524–36) as an exile on the Continent, for he found "not only that there was no room in my lord of London's palace to translate the New Testament, but also that there was no place to do it in all England". The copies of his first edition, begun in 1525 and completed in 1526, filtering into England hidden in bales of cotton, were burned at Paul's Cross at the instigation of William Warham, Archbishop of Canterbury, Cuthbert Tunstall, Bishop of London, Thomas Wolsey and Thomas More. He himself was burnt, after being strangled, in 1536 at Vilvorde, but not before he had prayed: "Lord, open the King of England's eyes"—a prayer answered only a year later by the royal recognition of the Coverdale Bible.

More and Tyndale engaged in mighty polemic. More wrote a *Dialogue concerning Heresies*. Tyndale replied with *An Answer unto Sir Thomas More's Dialogue*. More's rebuttal appeared in the form of his eight books of *Confutation of Tyndale's Answer* which occupy something like a thousand pages in the great Yale edition of More's *Works*. To our

175

modern way of looking at controversy, the language used by the two men seems unpleasant in the extreme. More was engaged in a fierce championship of the old religion, and in that championship was happy to pursue his opponent relentlessly with a barrage of polemical artillery. Tyndale did not spare his opponent, and the heat of the battle was fierce. It is astonishing that a man who carried such heavy burdens as More did could engage in so lengthy a refutation of reformist doctrine; but he shared the forboding of Erasmus and others of a coming widespread religious revolution, and felt it his duty to allow Bishop Tunstall to conscript him to undertake the suppression of heresy by a battle of books.

Here, then, are two sketches, terribly brief, of two men—both of them scholars enriched by the new learning; both of them deeply concerned to share with others their insights into God's truth; both of them saints, "far ben wi' God" (as the Scots would have it); both of them martyrs for the truth as they saw it, laying down their lives within a year of one another for Christ and conscience sake; but opposed, the one to the other, to the point of prolonged bitterness.

These two men pose a problem, a series of problems, which are not easy of solution. Today we do not engage in prolonged and bitter polemic—or at least not often. We do not kill one another—or at least very rarely—because of theological or intellectual differences. But divisions persist, separations continue, bitterness sometimes develops, and God's heart of love is grieved and the process of his cause is hindered.

Of course, it would be possible to say: "Let us love one another and leave it at that". But that might be to encourage a mere sentimentality and the sacrifice of truth on the altar of a sloppy *bonhomie*. This would be to do despite to the first of our texts, which ran: "Join the struggle in defence of the faith, the faith which God entrusted to his people once and for all". And that would not do, for truth *matters*. There is what the writer of the Pastoral Epistles calls a sacred 'deposit' of truth which it is for us to guard as a sacred thing and to pass on unimpaired to succeeding generations. "O Timothy, keep that which is committed to you"—all too easily it can be eroded. The Catholic faith, the faith of the Church down the ages, enshrined in holy Scripture and outlined in the Creeds and Councils of the Church, is a precious thing. "Keep that which is committed to you."

But what happens to this "sacred deposit" as age succeeds to age? There are accretions which sometimes dim the pristine beauty of the original revelation, and which do not accord with its main tenets. There are new insights and developments of truth, springing legitimately from

176

earlier revelations, which bear every mark of being the result of the activity of the Spirit of Truth. How do we distinguish these from the accretions which fetter and distort? There is the record of the persecution of good men by good men because of differences of belief and of insight. There is the legacy of hatreds which are not forgotten nor, as yet, forgiven, and which make an excuse for a continuation of differences today. It is against a somewhat sordid background that we must heed the injunction: "Join the struggle in defence of the faith entrusted to God's people once and for all".

Alongside this injunction from the Epistle of Jude we set another, from St. Paul: "Let us cease judging one another, but rather make this simple judgement, that no obstacle or stumbling-block be placed in a brother's way". St. Paul would be the first to affirm that truth matters. His controversy with St. Peter and with his own Jewish people, and his martyrdom for the truth's sake, prove that. But alongside it he puts the command not to judge any man—presumably in a spirit of pride or superiority or bitterness—but, rather, to see to it that no stumbling-block is put in his way. For, however much I may differ from my brother, however difficult it may be for me to see that his apprehension of truth can ever approximate to mine, he, like me, is "made in the image of God", and destined, in St. Paul's incomparable phrase, to "be shaped to the likeness of God's Son". We have a common destiny in the Mind of God.

We have looked at two great men, servants of God, at deep variance with one another, but both martyred in a cruel age for the truth as they saw it. What do they say to us? They say, surely, that truth, and not least the truth of the Christian revelation, matters, and matters deeply and intensely. They say, also, that love for one another matters, and matters as deeply and intensely.

If they, Thomas More and William Tyndale, could speak to us tonight, I think they might, in the light of the intervening centuries, tell us how to hold our texts together. They might say two things:—

1. See that you love one another fervently. Not sentimentally, God forbid, for that would be a travesty of Christian love. But with the love of brothers in Christ, redeemed, restored, forgiven through Him; one in baptism, one (soon, please God) in Eucharist, one in service. See that no obstacles be placed in a brother's way.

2. Be very sensitive to the movement of the Holy Spirit. He is the Spirit of Truth. He may come to us as a still small voice whose word we could all too easily miss. He may come to us like a rushing gale, blowing away our old conceptions, battering down our old regulations, giving us new insights, and all the time saying to us in his gentle way: "Remember, dear

177

child, you are only a babe. God is very big. You are very small. Walk humbly with your God and don't, please don't, put a stumbling-block in a brother's way."

ILLUSTRATIONS

facing page

1. Chelsea Old Church
   South aisle and More Chapel   18

2. Nave and Chancel   74

3. From the River   84

4. More Chapel arch and Chancel   98

5. Statue outside More Chapel   104

6. Looking West, More Chapel on the left   126

7. From Chelsea Embankment   148

8. Tenor bell, cast 1977   162

INDEX

Act of Supremacy, 13, 16, 24, 115

Ammonio, Andrew, 55

Anne Boleyn, 14, 56, 62, 89, 115, 130, 146

Arnold, Thomas, 17

Battle of books, 176

Bible, 42, 46, 123, 169, 174, 175

Bilney, 123

Bolt, Robert, 54, 56

Bunyan, 175

Cambrai, peace of, 55, 171

Campbell, W. E., 57

Canterbury, 173

Catherine (or Katharine) of Aragon, 14, 56, 62, 130

Cavendish, George, 55

Chelsea Old Church, 63, 68, 91, 103, 106, 136, 143, 164, 173

Church of Scotland, 17

Clerk, 56

Coggan, Archbishop Donald, 168

Colet, 40, 60, 113, 130, 174, 175

Conciliar Movement, 14

Convocation, 14, 16, 115, 167

Coverdale, 175

Cranmer, 42, 56, 57, 148

Cromwell, Thomas, 56, 84, 115

Ecumenical Movement, 87

Emperor Charles, 56

Erasmus, 13, 23, 24, 40, 48, 53, 62, 72, 73, 77, 88, 107, 113–4, 122, 124, 130, 133, 136–7, 141, 143, 153, 165, 171, 174, 175

Fisher, Archbishop Geoffrey, 168

Fisher, Bishop John, 15, 57, 147, 155

Forrest, John, 130

Frith, John, 55, 57

Gardiner, 56

Gillis, Peter, 171

Godly prince, 15, 18, 42

Grocyn, 54, 155, 174

Haereticus Molestus, 63

Harpsfield, Nicholas, 13

Harris, John, 156

Henry VIII, 14, 41, 42, 61, 63, 66, 78, 107, 124, 130, 138, 143, 155, 171

Holbein, 62, 71, 155, 171

International Commission of Anglican & Roman Catholic theologians, 168

Kant, Immanuel, 102

Knox, John, 16

Küng, Hans, 81

Laity, role of, 13, 16, 17, 28, 31, 142

Latimer, 174

Linacre, 54, 174

Lockey, 174

Luther, 41, 47, 60, 63, 107, 146, 156

Man for All Seasons, 54, 173

Manning, Cardinal, 17

More Chapel, Chelsea Church, 12, 76, 77, 79, 171

More, Dame Alice, 43, 56, 74, 151, 171

More, Margaret, 43, 57, 142, 147, 154

More, Thomas
   Oxford, 29, 39, 130, 141
   Lincoln's Inn, 56, 130
   Under-Treasurer, 29, 53
   Speaker of House of Commons, 29, 53, 55, 61, 107, 165, 171
   Lord Chancellor, 29, 47, 53, 62, 66, 107, 115, 116, 123, 130, 143, 171
   Field of Cloth of Gold, 30, 166
   Chelsea, 54, 61, 63, 72, 74, 77, 88, 107, 132, 135, 143, 151, 153–4
   Utopia, 29, 40, 55, 61, 62, 66, 72, 77, 84, 96, 107, 121, 136, 145, 151, 160
   Tyndale, 46, 47, 175
   Dialogues, etc., 47, 48, 54, 78, 146, 167, 175
   Tower, 33, 83, 96, 107, 109, 125, 131, 147, 174
   Canonisation, 92

Morton, Cardinal, 40, 122, 141, 173

National Portrait Gallery, 170, 173

Newman, Cardinal, 42

Oxford Reformers, 40

Pope, Alexander, 21

Pope John XXIII, 87, 89, 168

Pope Paul VI 87, 88, 101, 103

Pope, Thomas, 107, 109

Ramsey, Archbishop Michael, 87, 88, 103, 168

Rastell, William, 54

Reformation, 15, 49, 50, 83

Renaissance, 13, 23, 59, 174

Rich, 130

Roper, Margaret, 57, 115, 131

Roper, William, 54, 55, 96, 151

Royal Supremacy, 15, 16, 17

St. Francis, 135

Shakespeare, 24, 84, 175

Socrates, 102

Solomon, 65–66

Stapleton, Thomas, 17

Talbot, Monsignor, 17

Temple, Archbishop William, 135

Tewkesbury, John, 63

Tunstall, 46, 56, 57, 171, 175

Tyndale, 41, 46, 47, 55, 63, 97, 123, 146, 167, 174, 175

Warham, William, 175

Westminster Abbey, 21, 56

Westminster Hall, 100

Whitgift, Archbishop, 15

Wilson, Nicholas, 115

Wolsey, Cardinal, 24, 55, 61, 84, 175